# Lightworker

## Understand Your Sacred Role as Healer, Guide, and Being of Light

by

Sahvanna Arienta

New Page Books
A Division of
The Career Press
Pompton Plains, NJ

**LIGHTWORKER**

EDITED AND TYPESET BY NICOLE DEFELICE

Cover design by Lucia Rossman/Digi Dog Design

Printed in Canada

To order this title, please call toll-free 1-800-CAREER-1 (NJ) and Canada: 201-848-0310) to order using VISA or MasterCard, or for further information on books from Career Press.

The Career Press, Inc.
220 West Parkway, Unit 12
Pompton Plains, NJ 07444
www.careerpress.com
www.newpagebooks.com

**Library of Congress Cataloging-in-Publication**

CIP Data Available Upon Request.

# Dedication

To all the Lightworkers in my life, past, present, and future, thank you for being the light in the darkness.

## Acknowledgments

The information in this book will help so many people in the world who think that we have been abandoned by God, and thought that a Lightworker was someone who worked for an electrical company! I found writing a huge challenge. Thankfully, the universe brought the most brilliant editor, Katy Koontz, into my path and she gave the book the structure that it needed. Katy has the unique talent of keeping my voice alive as she organized my thoughts, corrected the grammar, and asked the questions that needed to be answered. She is also someone who "gets it," so to have an editor who understands my message and can translate it in a coherent way is a blessing all its own. Thank you, Katy. I also would like to acknowledge my Soul's Journey family. Your work and dedication to the light energy of the planet is miraculous. I am amazed at how you labor tirelessly, (sometimes at all hours of the night) for those in need. You practice honor, respect, and love for those who seek your guidance, you work as humble messengers of love and light, and that is rare. The world needs you and is a lighter place because of you. Thank you all for allowing me to live my dream. I am so grateful for each and every one of you. It is my wish that this book will alleviate some of the fear that we are surrounded with here on Earth; give some hope to a world that at times feels hopeless; and let those who feel isolated or outcast know that they belong and are needed in a big way.

# Contents

# Preface

> "The souls of people, on their way to Earth-life, pass through a room full of lights; each takes a taper—often only a spark—to guide it in the dim country of this world. But some souls, by rare fortune, are detained longer—have time to grasp a handful of tapers, which they weave into a torch. These are the torch-bearers of humanity—its poets, seers, and saints, who lead and lift the race out of darkness, toward the light. They are the law-givers and saviours, the light-bringers, way-showers, and truth-tellers, and without them, humanity would lose its way in the dark."
>
> —Plato

A Lightworker is a certain breed of soul. These are beings who have, throughout history, come to Earth incarnated as humans to enlighten, guide, and teach when needed. At the present time, a literal army of Lightworkers is arriving on the planet due to global issues that are rapidly spinning out of control and becoming a serious threat to humanity.

But this is no ordinary army. Lightworkers aren't all great spiritual gurus or even political leaders—they may be musicians or artists, shopkeepers or accountants, stay-at-home moms or homeless folks. Many forget their divine purpose once they get here, living among us unaware of who they really are or why they have come. Although it's not always obvious who these Lightworkers are, or easy to understand the qualities that make them different, one thing is certain: the Earth is more in need of these Lightworkers at this point in time than ever before.

## Why Now?

The population of the Earth, steadily increasing since the 1400s, has now reached more than 6 billion people. By 2040, experts say that number will reach 9 billion. As the Earth's population continues to increase, violence and crime have increased along with it. Darkness is beginning to overtake the Earth, annihilating its beauty. Humanity has become materialistic, power-hungry, and so filled with greed that, left to its own vices, mankind may ultimately destroy itself—and the Earth along with it.

Yet, there's reason for hope! Darkness fears one thing—light—because it simply cannot survive in light. So the only way to cast out these dark forces that threaten to take over our planet is to light up the Earth with an army of torch-bearers. These beings, the Lightworkers, are here to neutralize this darkness.

## Are You a Lightworker?

If this information seems vaguely familiar, it may be because you are a Lightworker. If so, you will recognize this truth on a soul level. That's the reason I wrote this book: to share my own experiences as a Lightworker and to reach out and offer support to other Lightworkers in hopes that they will recognize who they are and no longer feel alone, lost, and misplaced. Many Lightworkers struggle greatly in their lifetimes. In order to fully understand life on this Earth so they can serve humanity, Lightworkers must undergo life experiences that will give them an empathic understanding of others. Lightworkers are tempted, tested, and pushed into the dark. Many have had traumatic or unhappy lives. If you are a Lightworker, at times you may feel overwhelmed from casting light in a world that is cloaked in darkness and polluted with negativity. You may feel as though you are taking on the weight of humanity and can feel the pain of everyone on the planet at once. You may have prophetic dreams or even premonitions of worldwide disasters. You may even have had a near-death or out-of-body experience.

It is not uncommon for people who are not yet aware that they are Lightworkers to feel very lost and alone. These unaware Lightworkers may fall into a deep state of sadness, because they are not yet fulfilling their divine purpose. Some suffer depression, anxiety, or feelings of worthlessness. Some experience mood swings or even psychosomatic illness and anti-social behavior. In extreme cases, they have impulses to commit deliberate self-harm, such as cutting themselves or pulling out their hair. Many may try to medicate themselves, and in the process, become addicted to various substances.

Their egos may at times urge them to abandon their duties, but those who have been given divine gifts have an obligation to use them to enhance the greater good of mankind—an awesome responsibility.

My own dark period lasted almost 10 years. After my father died, my faith was greatly tested and I became unsure of my purpose. The road back to the light was long and painful, but this dark period gave me the time and space I needed to learn what I had to know so that I could continue my work here on Earth.

Most Lightworkers eventually rise above the darkness, growing spiritually in the process, but some will remain lost here on Earth without the vital knowledge of who they really are. If they can identify their divine purpose and begin the work they came here to do, much of their unhappiness and unpleasant feelings may dissipate and they will find focus in their lives. Eventually, they will come to understand that they are not meant to be damaged or tragic figures, but instead beacons of light for all mankind. Just one Lightworker can directly or indirectly enlighten thousands of people.

Often, Lightworkers' special gifts are labeled as "psychic powers." And as you will read later in this book, Lightworkers do indeed have various extra-sensory perceptions (including, in my case, seeing and communicating with the deceased). But it's vital to understand that though being a Lightworker does include using such psychic abilities, just "being psychic" is not enough. Lightworkers are put here to enlighten others in their spiritual paths, not just tell the future. Being a Lightworker is a calling, not a side show. The major difference between a psychic and a Lightworker is that a psychic may *tell* you your future, while a Lightworker will *guide* you into your future.

If you are feeing lost, but know deep inside you are here for a reason, you are experiencing an awakening of your dormant Lightworker soul. Now is the time to begin the journey of your life's work. As you do, you will find that you are not alone on your path.

The information and experiences you will read here are from my higher teachers, and my channeled information. This is not the ultimate truth, nor is it the only way to experience the spirit world. Everyone experiences it in different ways, and these are the things I was shown. It is my intention that, by reading this book, and discovering how to use your gifts to help others, you will become more aware of the divine love that constantly surrounds you, supporting and guiding you every step of the way.

# Introduction

I tried to imagine what our world would be like 20 years from now, then 40 years, and then finally, 100 years from now. Suddenly, I found my mind and my ethereal body in another place. In my vision, I followed a long road that seemed never-ending. Along the side of the road, I saw nothing but dried-out straw where I somehow knew was once a bountiful cornfield. I spotted my daughter holding a watering can further down the road, and ran to her so that we could water the field together. The faster I ran, the further away she was. I couldn't get to her in time. Was the message that what our children reap in the future, having been planted by the seeds of our past, will be irreversibly damaged?

Next, I had a vision of all humanity sitting on a shoreline and watching the last glimmer of light from the very last sunset on Earth dissipating on the horizon. We cried out for help as darkness fell upon us, and I wondered if our cries were being heard. My vision ended there, and I prayed for an answer. The next night, the answer came in a dream, and I was told that indeed our cries do not fall upon deaf ears and that help has arrived.

I wrote this book with the intention of letting the world know that the cries of humanity do not go unheard. True, the world as we know it is in crisis; but help is here. Hundreds of years of fear, greed, and hatred have tarnished our beautiful planet, and we have done it to ourselves. We can no longer ignore our own part in the collective. We have fed the discontent, the wars, the famines, and the darkness with our own hatred. Man was given a perfect world to inhabit; a place harmoniously aligned with all the love of our Source Creator, a place in which humanity could glory in. But somehow, the respect and appreciation for the utopia that we were given has practically vanished. Somewhere along the way, humanity lost its way. When mankind became aware of the rich treasures that our planet held, we decided that we needed to "own" them. Fear was used to manipulate, control, and possess. Then the perfect world of love and beauty became tarnished and skewed. Unconditional love was replaced by a fear-induced prison. Souls that were created with love and light became dark, heavy, and materialistic. Now here we are. New age messengers speak of the enlightenment and planetary shifts that are ongoing. This is not humanity suddenly waking up, taking notice of the trail of destruction that it has left and trying to undo the damage before that last glimmer of sunlight dissipates on the horizon. Rather, it is the answer to our prayers.

Decades ago, the word *Lightworker* was coined to mean someone who wanted to help to make the world a better place. A Lightworker was thought of as a person who had a higher calling to help people and the world itself through prayer, healing, meditation, energy work, and other spiritually related practices. The vague term intrigued me, and as I delved deeper into what was a mere label of sorts, I began to receive information from a higher source that brought the label into clear focus regarding who these unique souls were who had come to heal the planet. I received images of where they had descended from, and the different roles and divine purposes that they held. I was shown famous Lightworkers throughout history (for example, Mother Teresa, William Shakespeare), and how they contributed to the healing of our planet. These amazing beings of love and light were not merely those with some intangible calling who shouted from the mountain tops that they were here to bring salvation. They could indeed be the most ordinary, unobtrusive people; average people walking the Earth who were vessels for a light so brilliant that we had to shield our eyes, turn away, and allow them to go virtually unnoticed among us. These beings were souls who descended from glorious realms and had long-lost interest in the dense heaviness of the materialistic Earth plane.

The Lightworkers descended from places so magnificent that those of us here on Earth could not even begin to comprehend them. Why would Lightworkers choose to return to the Earth, which is so heavy with suffering and misery? The answer is that at the last hour of the last sunset, they have come to hear our cries. It is the Lightworkers' mission to lend their light to a planet that is heavy with fear and sickness. They have come before it is too late, and they are here to be of service to us. They speak out for those who have no voice, they create glorious works of art to beautify our planet, and they write music that elevates our spirits. They work unseen, lending their light energy by just agreeing to walk among us; they are the healers of our planet. While writing this book, I received information on the different realms, and the gifts that each Lightworker brings to Earth from his/her realm of origin. As I meditated, more and more specific information came through, and *Lightworker* was no longer a broad term or label, but a clear and defined role for these beings with different levels, intensities, and missions. The other information that I received was what I feel are the answers to what so many Lightworkers seek. I was shown the suffering that these sensitive beings endure by being present here on Earth—how they are misunderstood, ridiculed, sometimes persecuted; how they are cast into darkness, continuously being tested in their roles here as light bearers; how they have to painstakingly maintain their connection to the heavens, while still keeping two feet on the ground here on Earth. Because of their heightened sensitivities, they can literally feel trapped in the virtual torture chambers that are their physical bodies. Many unaware Lightworkers feel lost and isolated here on Earth, and many live each day with a yearning in the depths of their souls to go "home" even when they are already in their own house. I was given information to assist them in coping with the pain of trying to heal a damaged planet, and to live in a world to which they really don't belong; just as the Lightworker has been sent as an answer to humanity's cries for help. I hope that the information found in this book will provide the answers to the Lightworkers' pleas, and provide them with a life raft that will finally assist them in living in the space of love and healing that they themselves came here to deliver.

# Part 1:

# Discovering Your Origin

# 1

# We Are All Energy

In order to understand your Lightworker soul, we have to begin with where you come from—Source. Source is an all-knowing, all-powerful entity that dwells in every crevasse of the universe. Source is where we all come from, and where we all will eventually return.

Source is our Creator. It's Allah, Buddha, Yahweh, you, me—what is God's real name after all?

Source is also entirely neutral. The concept of good and bad does not exists within Source. Above all things, Source offers *unconditional love*. Regardless of your actions, beliefs, or faults, Source will love and accept all living creatures equally. Source is made up of energy.

You can think of it as somewhat like the electricity in your home: You can turn it on and it lights up your house, or you can shut it off and you will be sitting in darkness. But that electricity is always there, regardless of the position of your light switch. Everything you know is connected through this divine frequency. Basically, you can think of Source Energy as the common connection of the entire universe.

It is what connects every single thing in the entire universe with every single other thing in the entire universe—from huge things such as solar systems right down to the tiniest atom. It's in things that we ordinarily think of as living (man, animals, trees, and plants) as well as in things we don't normally think of as being alive (rocks, the ocean, the sky, and the stars).

Source Energy also isn't constrained by time. Within it, all things past, present, and future exist together, complete. That means that it also connects us with those who have died.

Because Source Energy penetrates all objects, psychics can receive information from the energy held in an object (an ability called *psychometry*). Metal is especially energy-absorbent.

As a psychic medium, I've done many readings for people who will hand me a ring or necklace that belonged to a relative who has departed. Within that object is residual energy left from the person who wore it.

## Reesa and Anna: Death Didn't Break Their Connection

When a young woman named Reesa came to see me for a reading one day, she placed a plain band of silver on my desk. "Can you give me any information on this ring?" she asked. As I held the ring, my hand became hot—almost as if I were holding my hand over an open flame. It tingled and burned. "I feel heat," I said impulsively, shocked at the intensity of the heat. As I began to ask my guides what the message was, I saw visions of flames and then flashes of a house on fire. I could hear the cries of children and the sounds of chaos. The visions, the sounds, and the extreme heat all together began to overwhelm me.

"There is a house fire related to this ring," I said.

"Yes," Reesa confirmed.

Then I heard the name "Anna," and suddenly the spirit of a young woman appeared standing beside Reesa. "Tell her I'm okay. Tell her everything is okay and to be happy," the spirit communicated.

"Anna is here," I told Reesa, not knowing who Anna was yet. "She says that she is okay, everything is okay."

Tears started to flow down Reesa's cheeks. Then she started to sob, placing her head in her hands. Empathetically, I could feel that these tears came from the deepest place in her soul, from wounds only this powerful kind of tears could heal. I placed the ring down and rubbed Reesa's shoulder, allowing her to cry. I could feel old internal wounds being healed as we sat together. When she could speak again, Reesa explained that she had had a twin sister named Roseanna who everyone in the family called Anna. Reesa and Anna's mother raised the girls by herself, and she had a long history of alcoholism. She spent many nights at the local tavern, leaving the girls home alone to care for themselves. Reesa and Anna had always looked out for one another, feeling that they basically had only each other to count on. When the girls were thirteen, the house's outdated electrical system shorted out one night, igniting a fire. As the girls slept, the house filled with smoke and was soon engulfed in flames. The fire department managed to rescue Reesa, who was badly burned. But Anna died trapped in the girls' attic bedroom, wearing the ring Reesa brought with her to the reading. Reesa's mother had given the ring to Reesa after Anna's funeral. Since that time, Reesa never took it off. She always assumed that this plain silver band was all that was left of her twin sister.

Reesa carried the scars of that night, both physically and spiritually. The pain and guilt of living through the fire and not being able to save her sister had plagued her for the past 18 years. For Reesa to hear Anna say that she was okay and that she wished Reesa happiness was an enormous weight being lifted off Reesa's back.

We continued to dialogue with Anna for a while, and Anna went on to say she had watched over Reesa for all these years. She told me of having been with Reesa when Reesa's son was born, and she how she had watched over her nephew as well. It was like a happy family reunion. Reesa was glad to know that Anna was happy in the spirit world and to hear that Anna had become the teacher she always dreamed of being—except that instead of teaching children on Earth, Anna now worked with children who have crossed over. Communicating like this takes a lot of energy for those in the spirit world, and the communication eventually began to fade as Anna was pulled back—

but not before she told us she would lovingly watch over her sister until they met again in the afterlife.

As the reading came to an end, the spirit of a brown spotted dog entered the room and sat at Reesa's feet. "We lost our springer spaniel in the fire, as well," Reesa said, wiping away tears.

"I think I just found her," I replied. "She's sitting at your feet!"

This story illustrates another quality of energy—it never dies, it just changes its form. Anna hadn't ceased to exist when she died in the fire. The energy within her just took a different form. And in this new form, she was still connected through Source Energy to Reesa and to her ring, which we could use to communicate with her. Because of these all-powerful energetic connections, we were able not only to contact Anna, but also to gain information that was extremely healing for Reesa. It was truly a magical experience for both of us.

## We're All in This Together

Within the Source Energy is the formula that set the Earth on its axis and allows it to constantly turn, that causes the sun to rise and set, and that gives us the ability to create life. It is the same energy that allowed Reesa and Anna's story to be accessed. The fact that the sun rises and sets each day is not random. All the little things we see each day and take for granted are precisely planned out by Source. Source also has intelligence, even though it doesn't have a physical body the way we do. To understand this, think for a minute about your own mind. It certainly has a physical form (your brain), but the brain is really only a transformer, an organ that computes information. Where does the information come from in the first place? Where do our thoughts originate? They all come from Source. And because we are all connected by Source Energy, we all share a small piece of its divine intelligence—and so we all have the power to access it whenever we wish to. Because this Source Energy is the life force that fuels the human experience, would it allow us to believe that we have the power to be "God-like"?

It is true that this energy in its purest, most evolved form is so awesome that it is beyond the comprehension and understanding of any human. But the gift every one of us is given when we take our first breath on this planet is to take in the smallest fraction of that power that we can imagine, and even with just that small fraction, we have the capacity to literally move mountains. Most of us do not use this power to its full potential because we don't believe we can or we don't have the desire. Lightworkers have come here expressly to harness this Source Energy and use it for good. But it is there for everyone, whether they realize it or not. Think of the story of the woman who lifted a car to save her child who was being crushed underneath. What gave this woman this sudden superhuman strength? The desire to save her child was so overpowering that it superseded the constraints of her physical body. The truth is that just as the woman lifted the car, we *can* literally move mountains if we have the desire and we believe we can.

Free will grants us the power to use this energy as we wish. Think of it this way: Imagine that your life is one big roadmap, and Source set you on a certain course. If you take an aerial view of the path that is set up for you, you see that there are turns, certain hazards, and dead ends. Each road has a different destination, passing different things to see, and leading those who travel it to encounter different people. But because you live on the ground (the Earth), you don't generally get to see this aerial view. So you cannot see what lies around the bend of each road as it twists and turns. That's where free will comes in. Source may have plotted a route for you, but free will gives you the ability to alter the course and choose which route to take, not knowing for sure exactly where the journey will lead you.

Each potential path holds the power to shape your life in different ways. And because we're all connected by Source Energy, as our individual paths and lives shift, we are also ever so slightly (and sometimes not so slightly) shifting the energy of everyone and everything else on the planet. Because we are all connected by the same energy, what affects one of us affects all of us. Here's another way to look at it: Think of all of us here on Earth as petals on one flower, and then think about how each petal contributes to the beauty of that flower. What if one petal becomes damaged? It would definitely change the flower's appearance, and if the damage was severe enough, the flower might not even survive. Being a part of the collective energy works the same way. One petal cannot be harmed without affecting the whole.

Within the collective, each and every one of us is significant to the balance of Source Energy. As we begin to understand this concept more fully, we can see that Source Energy actually requires and actively seeks balance to keep all the forms of life that it contains in perfect alignment. Because Source is perfection, when the energy that it is made up of becomes unbalanced, *everything* ends up wobbling!

## Light Energy: The Power to Heal

One type of energy that Source Energy contains is light energy—all the free-flowing beauty of the universe. Light energy doesn't weigh us down; it lifts our spirits and elevates our general state of being. This is the type of energy Lightworkers use to heal the world, although you don't have to be a Lightworker to use light energy. One way we can experience this on a tangible level here on Earth is through appreciating the beauty of nature. Another is through loving others. Yet another is creating art or music. What all of these experiences have in common is emotion. We have the power through our minds to actually manifest light energy through what we think (our thoughts) and how we think it (our intentions). Our minds are directly connected to Source. Our brain is the computer that interrupts and stores the information. When we do manifest light energy through our minds, the effects resonate throughout the universe like ripples in a pond after a stone is tossed into it. The Lightworker is composed of more light energy than most beings and also has the ability to focus this light energy like a laser beam to protect and heal (using various forms of energy medicine, such as Reiki, therapeutic touch, or even acupuncture).

A perfect example of how this works involves a story about my mother, who has always searched out new ways to access the power of Source Energy. Back in the 1960s, when she worked as a second grade teacher in a Catholic school, she even found a way to incorporate her love of the mystical into the classroom without anyone else on the staff, including the principal, knowing that she was reaching beyond the usual lesson plans. She was like an undercover metaphysical agent. When a child in her classroom was sick, for example, she'd instruct the children to sit in a circle on the floor. "We're going to have a prayer circle to make Johnny better," my mom would whisper. "I want you all to picture Johnny inside a warm, bright, white light, surrounded by healing energy. Then picture him well and playing kickball in the schoolyard with you all." Because she called it a prayer circle instead of a healing circle, it seemed quite natural to the children.

When the sick child would recover quickly and return to school, the children would be so proud to see the results of their work. She always felt that children were the most powerful of manifesters, because their minds were so open and unaffected by what society tells us is and is not possible. She warned me never to take away a child's belief in Santa Claus, fairy tales, or magic, because those beliefs only lent themselves to a belief in bigger, more powerful things—such as the power to heal. The ability to believe is the most powerful gift we have, she told me, and children have this gift naturally. One of the boys in her class suffered from childhood leukemia, and my mother conducted daily healing sessions for him with the class for weeks. After two months of treatment, the boy returned to school. The doctors had not expected him to make it, and his full recovery was nothing short of miraculous. My mother cried tears of joy, seeing him running and playing kickball in the schoolyard again. And she was convinced that the second grade healing circle was imperative to his recovery, proving that miracles *do* occur if we can just access light energy from Source.

## Dark Energy: The One Thing Light Energy Can't Exist Without

We may tend to think the dark energy is "bad," which is not exactly true. Without nightfall, the daybreak would never come, and without sorrow, we would not truly appreciate the feeling of joy. To think that Source is all light would be a misconception. Because Source Energy is neutral and all-encompassing, it must also include the darkness. Source Energy is a double-edged sword that can penetrate our lives in different ways. Our free will allows us to wield it in whatever way we choose, and most of us chose to use it for different things at different times (even if we're not aware that we're actually making that choice at the time). Source accepts both light and dark equally, wrapping them both in a blanket of unconditional love and support—because unconditional love is all Source knows. Dark does not necessarily mean evil (although there *is* evil within the universe). Dark is a state of being, like the grief that we endure when we lose a loved one or the feeling of being lost and alone when nothing seems to be going right in our lives. Evil, on the other hand, is dark energy that is acted on with intention (such as committing murder out of feelings of hate or rage).

One of the important values in dark energy is that it can push us, motivating us to seek out the light. It's like being in the shade of a tree on an early spring afternoon. We can stay there for only so long before we begin to feel cold. And then we want to step out of the shadows and into the sunlight to feel warm and energized. So the dark, kept in the proper perspective, deserves our respect and appreciation.

Both dark and light energy are equally accessible to us here on Earth, and we can access the power of either with our intentions to heal or harm. Intentions are the originators of our actions and have a much greater affect than most people realize. So, for example, if someone were to start a foundation for increasing awareness about environmental causes, and if one person was informed by the foundation, then the founder's intention would have been achieved—even if the foundation were to go under the very next day. The energy around the foundation would be light energy, even though it may look on the outside as though the foundation was a failure.

On the other hand, if someone were to perform a good deed but does it begrudgingly, then the true feelings under the action, the person's resentment or malice, will taint the energy around the deed. The person will be bringing dark energy to the deed—even though on the outside it looks as though the person has done a good thing. The intention affects the energy more than the action. Because Source Energy lives in all of us and connects all of us, intention, not action, is what creates the biggest shifts in Source Energy. Action can shift energy, of course—we live in a physical world, after all. But it's the *intention* behind the action that matters most. Our world is more energetic than most of us realize. And just because we can't see this with our physical eyes doesn't mean it isn't so. (Case in point: You can't see gravity either; you can only see its effect.) You can boil all of this down into the wise old adage: we reap what we sew.

In this manner, we are constantly directing Source Energy (be it light or dark) into tangible form through our thoughts, actions, and most of all, intention. We can manifest consciously or unconsciously, which means our intentions have this effect whether we realize it or not. If we are aware of how this works, then it's easier to change our thoughts. Just as positive, loving thoughts (light energy) through the ripple effect of our intentions manifest good, negative thoughts and emotions (dark energy) manifest negative outcomes. They bring destruction, hatred, sickness, and suffering—all in the natural course of the energetic flow. Think of it as a simple consequence rather than divine retribution (just as you receive a shock when you stick your finger in a light socket—the jolt isn't delivered because you deserve it). So if what you experience comes from the energy that you put out there, light energy creating positive experiences and dark energy creating negative experiences, then the question arises, from what type of energy do you want to create your reality?

## Letting in More Light

Your thoughts not only change your own personal reality, but that of the entire universe. Each time we send out a good thought or blessing, we shift the universal energy. Within each prayer is the power to heal the world (just as every oak tree you've ever seen, no matter how big it is, grew from a relatively humble-looking acorn). Each time we love another living creature, we tip the scales of the universal energy toward the light. In this way, our positive thoughts accelerate the positive energy of the universe. This is the goal of the Lightworker.

Here's another way to look at that process: each time we take part in all that is good, we perform an act of God. Most of us have grown up hearing that we have been made in God's image. The true meaning of that isn't physical, but metaphysical—the truth it reflects is that the power of God lives inside each and every one of us. Many of us go through our entire lives without knowing how powerful we really are. It's easy to see how this can happen, though, because we're used to thinking that action is the hard part. But once you realize the true power of intention, you make an important shift in perception. You start to see the nuances of this truth, as well, that acts of kindness performed robotically or in a self-serving manner will never achieve an energetic shift.

Without the realization that all good deeds must be carried out with the purest of intentions for the greater good of all mankind, you will never create the shifts in your own life that you desire. Incorporating more light energy from Source into our lives requires making conscious choices about our thoughts and our general state of being. Because every emotion translates into energy, the more we allow light energy to flow throughout our lives with positive emotions, the more light we create and the happier and more fulfilled we become. The aware Lightworker will naturally gravitate toward this, because that is the very reason all Lightworkers are here. But Lightworkers who are unaware of their true spiritual nature can have greater challenges with this. They may feel excessively drained or exhausted because their sensitivity absorbs dark energies like a sponge. They often feel as though they are in the middle of a tug of war. It's not easy being a Lightworker! Being ever-vigilant in making conscious choices to attract and reflect light is extremely important. Everyone can learn to do this, even those who are not Lightworkers, because this light energy is available to all. In fact, people who do not harbor much light energy because they feel depressed or stagnated can learn to draw more light energy into their lives to lift their depression and dissipate their lethargy. This will bring them more vitality, better physical health, and an overall better state of mind—all of which will help them manifest the life they were put here for. They may have the million-dollar mansion or the 100-foot yacht, but it will be the life they came here to live. This will then add more light to the collective.

## Oceans of Emotions

Whether you consider yourself a Lightworker or not, you can create more light energy by living in a state of positive emotion. Examples of these light-inducing emotions include:

- Love.
- Gratitude.
- Forgiveness.
- Kindness.
- Acceptance.
- Generosity.
- Tolerance.
- Understanding.

Conversely, we create dark energy when we live in a state of negative emotion. Examples of negative emotions that create dark energy are:

- Hatred.
- Fear.
- Intolerance.

* Greed.
* Apathy.
* Lust.
* Envy.

Drawing from the emotions that are made up of light energy can be very difficult or very easy. It's simply a matter of using our free will to align with the light—and then making choice after choice that will keep us in that alignment. Getting off course every once in a while is to be expected. But those who are able to stay in the light most of the time can do so only by using the power of their intention to consistently make that choice.

My client Marian learned this after her 27-year-old son, William, was found dead. She described him as a smiling boy who grew up loving baseball and collecting frogs down at the lake. William had idolized his father and wanted to grow up to be an auto mechanic, just like his Dad. But William's father wasn't a happy person like his son. He battled addiction his entire life. He had been in in-patient treatment centers, 12-step programs, and support groups, and had been in recovery several times—but he always fell back into using drugs. He seemed at war with addiction and was never able to overcome it. When William was 16, his father took a bus to New York City to buy drugs and never returned. He was missing for a week before the police identified his body and called to inform William's mother that her husband had died on a bus from a bad batch of heroin.

After his father passed, William began to change. During the next several years, he became angry, felt victimized, and blamed others when things didn't go his way. He eventually moved out on his own. A few years later, he was found dead, alone in his apartment. The cause wasn't immediately apparent, and Marian came to see me to get some answers about what had happened. I linked with William in spirit, and he showed me an image of a boy and his father running and happily playing Frisbee. I explained the scene to Marian and she explained that William and his father played ball and Frisbee many times at the neighborhood park. Then, like a flash, what I saw changed. I was shown images of dark creatures and what looked like demons struggling to be freed. It immediately came to my mind that William had fought his father's demons. He was showing me that, like his father, he had lost the battle. I gave Marian the information that William died of a drug overdose, just like his dad. She seemed shocked, yet when the autopsy was completed; it showed that William had purposely overdosed on sleeping pills prescribed by his doctor.

What happened to the smiling boy Marian once knew? What went wrong? William let the pain and tormented energy of his father penetrate his own life. Why did he choose to take on his father's demons instead of separating himself from his father? He could have just as easily learned the lesson that drugs will kill you. Instead, he never took responsibility for his own life. He dwelled on the negatives so much that they became his dominant energy. He allowed the same dark energy that had surrounded his father to penetrate his own life, eventually destroying him.

William always had a choice, but he didn't realize it. Source never stopped giving him unconditional love and support. He could have made a conscious decision to use light energy, like what he had experienced as a happy child playing Frisbee with his Dad. But when his dark moods started to overwhelm him, he used his free will to turn away from the light instead of using his free will to reach out to the light to help him. But when William chose to swallow that fistful of pills, it didn't release him from the dark energy that surrounded him in life. Because our essence is created by energy, the energy we harbor doesn't change when we depart this lifetime. We carry it with us when we cross over. And it makes quite a difference to our transition. Just as it does when we are alive, our energy dictates where we go and what we do after we pass. And because we are still connected to everyone and everything through Source Energy, our dominant energy—light or dark—continues to affect the balance of what happens here on Earth. Now let's take a closer look at dark energy and what specific steps we can take to free ourselves from it, as well as how Lightworkers can help free others—both living and dead—from dark energy's grip.

# 2

# Casting Light on Dark Energy

As you will recall from the last chapter, Source is made of completely neutral energy—both dark and light. The energy it is composed of is transmutable and changes from light to dark and all points in between. Being a small spark of Source Energy, you control the hue of the energy in your own personal energy field, which has a place in the collective (like one dot of color or a pixel in an entire photograph made up of millions of pixels). Because we are all a part of Source, we need to embrace the dark with the same unconditional love we would the light.

Remember, dark energy is all about negative thoughts and emotions—it's not the same thing as evil.

Dark energy kept in proper balance should never invoke fear. In fact, as you'll read later in this chapter, properly managing dark energy can *accelerate* your spiritual growth.

We will all find ourselves in the dark at one time or another. Because every thought we have and every action we take transmutes into energy, we cannot avoid dark energy. The times when you are lonely, or when you feel sadness or grief, are all times you will be harboring an excess of darkness in your personal energy field. If you learn how to live in it, processing it so that it's transient, instead of allowing the dark energy to root itself and become firmly entrenched, the dark energy can indeed become healing and empowering.

## The Effect of Dark Energy on the Earth

Because dark energy comes directly from Source, it is available throughout our universe and is just as easily accessed as light energy. In fact, at this time, dark energy is more accessible than light energy because the energetic scales of our planet are unbalanced in favor of dark energy. This excess of dark energy is allowing the dark to overshadow the light to the point of being destructive. Wars, crime, natural disasters, plagues, famines, as well as general discontent will all continue to increase if the darkness is not controlled soon. Mankind is at risk of destroying itself (and the Earth) as it continually becomes materialistic, power-hungry, and filled with ego-driven, negative emotions.

Most of these negative emotions boil down to one basic emotion—fear. Fear can mask itself as greed (a fear of lack), jealousy (a fear of loss), and hatred (a fear of unconditional love).

❋ ❋ ❋ ❋

Although many people don't realize it, we live in a world that actually thrives on fear. For example, the media—particularly in advertising and marketing—is filled with fear. Even the simplest cosmetics commercial touting ageless beauty is designed to instill within us a fear of our own mortality. Mankind has learned to use fear as a tool to manipulate and mold humanity as a whole. Until we begin to step out of this place of fear and into enlightenment, the darkness will increase.

The population explosion is another marker of the increase in darkness. The planet's population has been steadily increasing since the 1400s, and experts say that by 2040, the global population will reach nine billion. This may, at first, be seen as a positive—the result of modern medicine that lengthens our lifespan. But that's only partly true. This population increase is also a direct result of a lack of spiritual awareness of collective souls on the planet. As we became more and more fear-based and less spiritual, we create a vicious cycle of souls who keep recycling back to Earth in order to fulfill their attachment to material desires and addictions.

A lack of spirituality and faith has caused many souls to refuse to leave the Earth, clinging in fear to the physical world with the idea that this is where they will find contentment and happiness. Many continue to return over and over again in a misguided attempt to satisfy an insatiable craving for physical pleasures. This adds to the Earth's dark energy, and most of these souls will only pick up more darkness during their incarnations. When we see a significant decline in births, it will be a result of spiritual enlightenment throughout the planet.

Unfortunately, that could take hundreds of years.

## David's Story: Disincarnates Who Bring Darkness

Some souls who die simply refuse to move on, wandering among us with nowhere to go. Others cross over and sit in the next level of consciousness and wait to return to Earth, causing an overload of dark energy wherever they are. This creates a weight of dark energy that is basically smothering the Earth. Many Lightworkers are now coming forward to rescue these spirits. Some of these Lightworkers call themselves paranormal investigators or even ghost hunters, but their job is the same—helping to free these souls who are stuck here, fearful of moving on, who are contributing to the dark energy of the planet. David's story is a good example of how a creative solution may be required to help free these trapped souls.

David, a family friend of mine, was thrilled to find his dream house after months of searching. He immediately fell in love with a house built in 1800, with its old-world charm and double-sided fireplace. An in-law suite on the third floor would be perfect for David's aging mother, Claire. The house needed work, but David got it for a good price at an estate sale and was convinced it was the deal of a lifetime. And because he was a contractor, he knew exactly how to go about restoring the house to its original magnificence. But David's wife Julia had some reservations. She told David that even though the house was stately and the property exquisite, she felt the home had a strange "feeling" to it.

Not long after they moved in, Claire began experiencing some health issues. She began feeling drained, and after a few months, became so lethargic that she isolated herself upstairs, barely interacting with anyone. This was very unusual for Claire, who was normally very outgoing.

In addition, David and Julia were trying to start a family, and with each passing month they became more disappointed that they were not able to conceive. As Julia became increasingly discouraged by their infertility, she began experiencing anxiety attacks. With all the stress, the couple began to bicker and quarrel. All their plans of living happily ever after were fading fast.

When Christmas came around, Julia wanted to host an old-fashioned Victorian Christmas gathering. I was thrilled to be invited, and we all got to string popcorn for the perfectly decorated eight-foot Christmas tree. Throughout the evening, I couldn't help but notice the shadowy spirit of a hunched-over female figure wandering the room. She looked as though she was hovering over the party-goers, trying to listen in on conversations. I even caught a glimpse of her face and discovered that she looked quite prim and proper, with her hair pulled back tightly. I smiled and acknowledged her, but when I tried to connect with her, her energy seemed very agitated. All I got in response was a voice asking in an annoyed tone, "Who are you?" So I decided to ignore the spirit and speak to David about her later.

After New Year's Eve, I contacted David and let him know about the woman at the party. David invited me back to investigate, telling me that Julia had suspected all along that a presence occupied the home. Soon after I arrived, we all sat in a circle. I lit a white candle and blessed the process as we started to call in the spirit. As we began the séance, I saw the same woman from the party standing behind David's mother. I asked her name and telepathically heard her say, "Emily." Emily explained that she lived in the house with her roommate "Charlotte," referring to Claire. Emily appeared next to Claire and was definitely attached to her—and most of all attached to the house. She related in no certain terms that she was an agoraphobic (someone who has a fear of the outdoors) and that she hadn't ever left the house during the last 10 years of her life.

When I relayed this information to David, he said that when he moved in, he found hoarded items from the previous owner, such as old magazines and newspapers that were up to fifteen years old! Because it was an estate sale, David didn't get much information about the previous owner. All he knew was that the person had been an eccentric elderly woman who had passed away. Her family, who lived out of state, sold the home using a realtor service.

Emily was afraid to leave the house, and when the new owners moved in, she was confused and scared. She clung to Claire and insisted that they were childhood friends. Apparently, she had mistaken David's mother for a childhood friend named Charlotte.

I tried to explain to Emily that Claire was not her childhood friend and that she was free to leave the house now. Still, Emily would not hear of leaving. Just as when she was in physical form, Emily still suffered from agoraphobia and was fiercely attached to the house. Her mental condition was not improving in the spirit world, and it was clear to all of us that she needed help.

I went home that night and conversed with my guides, who had a unique solution. They decided to enlist help from the spirit world to energetically recreate the beautiful home Emily loved and felt safe in. The plan was then to gradually introduce themselves to Emily and move her to the energetically duplicated environment, where she would be comfortable. They told me they would work with her mental issues once she adjusted in the spirit world. My guides found Emily's loved ones from the spirit world (even the real Charlotte showed up) and little by little, they moved Emily into her new energetic home. As Emily became happy, her energy was transmuted into light—and the dark energy from her unhappiness was lifted from David's family. Claire's health and energy level improved, and she soon went back to her weekly bingo games at the local senior citizen's center. And six months after the spirit rescue, Julia became pregnant. By transmuting Emily's unhappiness and lifting her up spiritually, we all contributed in making the Earth a lighter place.

## Damage Control: Deflecting Dark Energy

With an ongoing accumulation of the dark energy on the planet, Lightworkers have been activated to return here to balance out the energy. Lightworkers descend to Earth from above, one by one, naturally harboring an excess of light energy, which begins to tip the scales back into energetic balance. The Lightworker's main purpose is transmuting the dark energy just by agreeing to be present here on Earth, but the Lightworker army has a natural inclination to be of service to the general population as well. Like a chain reaction, one Lightworker's energy can resonate into the universe and enlighten thousands. And when a Lightworker takes action by teaching or guiding, this action then accelerates the balancing of the Earth's energy.

As a Lightworker, you must first learn to identify dark energy by the way it makes you feel cold, heavy, and weighed down—before you can learn how to deflect it. You can feel these reactions physically, emotionally, and spiritually. Some symptomatic reactions to dark energy may include:

- Excessive fatigue.
- Anxiety.

- Headache.
- Backache.
- Stomachache.
- Depression.
- Feeling alone or isolated.

When you recognize what is happening, it's vitally important to try to keep your outlook as bright and positive as possible to deflect as much of the dark energy as you can before it has a chance to do more damage. Only when a Lightworker becomes stagnant and is not able to process this dark energy does it begin to overshadow his or her light and eventually overpower it. This can happen very easily if the Lightworker is not aware of the light- and dark-inducing emotions and how to balance energy in a world that is already unbalanced—not an easy feat.

Lightworkers who don't understand what is happening can find that as this dark energy deepens, it affects their actions. Addictions, antisocial behaviors, and committing acts of self-harm are common signs of an excess of dark energy. Lightworkers heavy with dark energy repeatedly get into unhealthy relationships, all in an effort to quell the feelings that these energies induce. Sadly, all this does is add more dark energy to the Lightworker's personal energy field, and as he or she spirals deeper, escape becomes more difficult, as if the Lightworker were mired in quick sand.

## Why Lightworkers Need Dark Energy Sometimes

At times, Lightworkers will find that, although the effects of dark energy may not feel good, limited periods of darkness can be beneficial. Dark energy has its time and place in a Lightworker's journey. Dark energy based on your emotions will force you to retreat and can indicate a period of healing. Within each and every one of us is a soft, soothing, dark space where we can be tucked in tightly and take the time to convalesce. Because we are never alone, our guides and loved ones in the spirit world will accompany us there while we repair our spirits after trauma.

The grief we suffer when a loved one transitions into the spirit world, for example, will often put us into a dark place deep inside ourselves. Feelings of sadness, isolation, and emotional pain (all dark-energy-inducing emotions) are to be expected, but also be aware that during this time, you will be guided through the internal darkness to a place where you can work through the grieving process and heal your energy. Because Lightworkers are naturally composed of more light than dark energy, it's perfectly okay to settle into the darkness for a period of time. Once the healing process is complete, you will emerge back into the light in a state of acceptance.

Another reason all Lightworkers will become pushed, pulled, or tempted into the darkness at times has to do with their ability to be of service to those in need. At times, Lightworkers require the soul experience of being thrown into the darkness so they can learn how to navigate around that darkness in order to understand, assist, and enlighten others who are trapped there.

For the unaware Lightworker who has not discovered his or her true path, this can be a scary, painful, and confusing experience. At times, Lightworkers can get lost in the darkness, often wondering why they have to suffer more than most people, and why the dark seems to follow them everywhere they go. Yet, like a lifeguard, the Lightworker will dive into a sea of darkness and rescue those who are drowning—being able to relate and empathize with others requires going into the water and getting wet.

Another benefit of these dark periods is rapid soul progression. During dark times, the universe presents us with one or more major life lessons. As we experience them, we overcome karma, complete soul contracts, and transmute dark energy, further elevating our spiritual status and that of the collective energy. After all, a Lightworker who combats dark energy in his or her own life is actually servicing the entire collective by transmuting dark energy into light. Helping others through your own personal experiences with darkness is not the only way to shift dark energy to light. Finding and dedicating yourself to causes that have personal significance is a wonderful way to transmute dark energy. Even a simple prayer for others, a thought of love and light, will begin to transmute the dark energy around you.

On a final but important note, please remember that as super-sensitive beings, Lightworkers may absorb the dark energy of those around them or even of the collective and feel the effects. In this way, the suffering they feel may not always belong to them. It is important to be aware of this collective dark energy so you won't be blindsided by it—especially because as a Lightworker, you are here to balance and transmute the dark energy for the entire planet.

3

# Discovering Your Origin

Our universe has many dimensions of existence, of which the Earth plane is only one. We call these dimensions *planes*, which is just another term for *worlds*. Layers upon layers of energetic worlds we cannot see from our perspective in the physical exist. These worlds include places so glorious that only beings of pure light, love, and wisdom (including ascended masters such as Christ or Buddha) reside there. Although each soul's destiny is to reach these "higher" planes, it doesn't happen quickly or automatically. Each plane has lessons a spirit must master before it can move on to the next plane. When a spirit has learned enough to move ahead, its newfound enlightenment and light energy expand. This increases the spirit's vibration (or frequency) until eventually it ascends to the next level. As we ascend higher and higher through these energetic worlds, we become more pure and light-filled, and ultimately we become one with Source. These higher realms are where the Lightworkers come from. It can take many lifetimes and a lot of work to accumulate the amount of light energy needed to ascend to these higher realms. An incarnation on Earth is best seen as merely an apprenticeship to a higher school of learning.

## Where Are These Other Worlds?

When I say that Lightworkers come from higher worlds, I don't mean that these worlds are literally above us the way the sky is above us. These other planes are actually all around us, co-existing in the same space as we do in the universe—but they occupy different vibrational levels. To understand this more easily, imagine the blades of a ceiling fan. When you turn on the fan, the blades begin to spin, and soon they are going so fast that you cannot see them anymore. The blades are still there, but your physical eye can't perceive them. Similarly, the wings of a hummingbird flutter so quickly that they seem invisible. It's the same with the higher realms. They vibrate at a much faster frequency than we do here on Earth. This means that right now you are sharing space with other realms that are full of life. If you were consciously aware of the non-physical world around you all the time, you would be overwhelmed by the spirits, entities, and life forms that surround you. As you begin to live your physical incarnation in a more spiritually based way, your energetic self becomes more light-filled and vibrates at a higher frequency, allowing you to begin to ascend up the realms to the higher planes. But remember, this isn't a quick trip! It could take hundreds of lifetimes or thousands of years to achieve enough spiritual growth to ascend to the higher realms. Lightworkers have worked hard at living in a place of unconditional love and so they have more light energy. They have long ago lost interest in the physical world and have no reason to return to the darkness of the Earth plane. Yet it is simply in each Lightworker's nature to feel the duty to return and share some of his or her light in order to balance the Earth plane's energy and heal the planet. They agree to return to enlighten humanity.

## The Seven Planes

Seven major planes exist between the physical Earth plane and Source, and each plane or realm is unique. The Earth plane (the first plane) is the heaviest and holds the most darkness, while Source (the seventh plane) is the lightest and has the most light-filled, loving frequency of all. Because the Earth plane is very dense and heavy, it holds the least amount of light energy. The Astral plane is a buffer zone between Earth and the higher realms. These are very different from the higher planes.

Lightworkers' souls come from the third plane on up through the seventh plane. Knowing which of those planes you as a Lightworker have descended from is valuable because it will help define your role as a light bearer here on Earth. What follows is a discussion of the individual planes, including what occurs on each and what type of Lightworker is associated with each. I'll also include examples of famous Lightworkers throughout history who have descended from each plane—but please remember that you do not need to achieve any amount of fame or notoriety with your Lightwork. You do not have to perform your Lightwork on any grand scale at all. Lightworkers from every plane may go totally unnoticed by the world, yet still contribute to the light energy of the Earth plane. As you read the description of each plane, one realm will probably resonate more strongly with you, revealing the true nature of your Lightworker soul. This knowledge is vital, because to understand where you're going, you must understand where you come from.

## The First Plane: Earth

The Earth plane is the first plane. As you've already read, this plane contains the most amount of dark energy of all the realms we will discuss. The Earth plane is made up of the material, and its frequency is heavy and dense. Although it can be regarded as a place of struggle, it is also a place of education. This is where we should be completing life lessons and balancing out our karma. We may take eons to achieve this, especially for those who refuse to let go of the material. These souls keep incarnating on Earth because they have not managed to raise their light energy and instead harbor a great deal of dark energy. These people have very little spirituality and live a fear-based existence. The spirit that is attached to the Earth plane may:

- Be very materialistic.
- Be self-centered.
- Have self-esteem, trust, and boundaries issues.
- Have very little faith or trust in anyone or anything.
- Experience health issues associated with sciatica and lower back, constipation, hemorrhoids, adrenal glands, prostate, varicose veins, and feet.

- Experience extreme mood swings.
- Develop addictions to sex, food, or alcohol.
- Never feel safe.
- Live a fear-based existence.

### What may help enlighten the Earth-plane spirit?

In order to create more light in your personal energy field, it is very important to focus on your general state of being. Staying within the light-inducing emotions (such as gratitude, generosity, and unconditional love) will automatically raise your light energy. Developing your spirituality and belief system will also accelerate your spiritual progress. You can also practice the following:

- Connecting with nature by spending time outdoors.
- Praying for the greatest good of all mankind daily.
- Being of service to others.
- Developing a stronger sense of faith.
- Developing a sense of spirituality, taking a spiritual class, or participating in spirituality-based activities.
- Staying within light-inducing emotions, such as love, gratitude, and forgiveness.

## The Second Plane: The Astral

The Astral is like a between-world where souls can still connect easily with the Earth plane and yet at the same time be in the spirit world. People in the physical are permitted to travel here as well. Anytime you have a dreamtime visit of a deceased loved one, you have met on the Astral plane. Spirits can also use the Astral plane to recreate life on Earth or to create environments that gratify the desires of their earthly life. This plane reminds me of my Aunt Rose, who always dreamt of a little house in heaven where she and her mother could plant flowers and finally be together again. The Astral plane provides a buffer zone between a dense Earth plane, heavy with dark energy, and the higher realms of pure love, light, and wisdom. The Astral plane also provides very pleasant surroundings for convalescing after perhaps being traumatized by physical death. Loved ones and spirits from higher realms may come down and counsel a spirit who is spending time on the Astral plane adjusting. For many reasons, spirits may choose to stay in the Astral plane. Some may stay there hundreds of Earth years before deciding to reincarnate on the Earth. Or they may stay long enough to increase their light energy enough to move to a higher realm, where they can finally become Lightworkers.

## The Third Plane

"Darkness cannot drive out darkness; only light can do that.

Hate cannot drive out hate; only love can do that."

—Dr. Martin Luther King, Jr.

When a spirit finally makes the decision to let go of all material attachments, the spirit will ascend to the third plane, where that spirit will now harbor enough light energy to be considered a Lightworker. Here, spirits finally begin to understand the concept of spiritual progress. They understand that they are journeymen in their spiritual quest and can choose one of two paths—to reincarnate back to Earth and continue their apprenticeship there, or to stay in the third plane and act as a guide for those on the Earth plane. Spirits who decide to stay in this plane and act as spirit guides for those on Earth may assist one person or several. Either way, the job is a win/win for all parties involved. Being a spirit guide is part of the evolutionary process for these spirits, and it helps increase their light energy. Spirits gain knowledge and wisdom through their work as guides. Spirits who leave the third plane and return to Earth display strong intuitive powers and know things instinctually. They are like human lie detectors that have a deep understanding of not only what is being said, but what is not being said. They have strong gut instincts and yearn to speak the truth. They always seek justice and can be vigorous advocates for those in need. Lightworkers from the third plane can:

- Have powerful intuitive feelings.
- Have a strong sense of self discipline.
- Have a strong sense of justice.
- Be an advocate for those in need.
- Have a strong urge to speak out when they see injustice.
- Be the one to organize rallies and gather the people for the sake of humanity.
- Risk everything for something or someone they believe in.

Lightworkers from the third plane make excellent judges, lawyers, politicians, police officers, teachers, social workers, non-profit or charitable foundation organizers, and intuitive advisors.

**Third-plane Lightworker facts:**

*Color*: golden yellow

*Element*: fire

*Sensitive body parts*: stomach, liver, gallbladder, spleen, adrenal glands

*Basic strengths*: self-esteem, vitality, forcefulness, intuition, insight, strong will, discipline

*Gemstones and crystals*: citrine, jasper, topaz

*Flower essences*: chamomile, goldenrod, pink yarrow

*Essential oils that soothe*: black pepper, ginger, peppermint

*Balancing foods*: complex carbohydrates (such as whole grains, beans)

**Famous third-plane Lightworkers:**

Dr. Martin Luther King, Abraham Lincoln, Oprah Winfrey, Joe Clark, Nelson Mandela, Father Damien, Rosa Parks, Clara Barton.

## The Fourth Plane

"Every beauty which is seen here by persons of perception resembles more than anything else that celestial source from which we all are come."

—Michelangelo

Upon arriving at the fourth plane, a spirit will enter into a dimension where the beauty of sight is not possible for the human eye to process. The quality of sound is so clear and pure that that it is beyond words and the brilliance of the light energy is incomprehensible to us here on Earth. The fourth plane is a place of glorious love and light. All the beauty of sight and sound are here.

Lightworkers who descend from the fourth plane work from a place of pure love and healing light. These Lightworkers bring kindness, compassion, and hope to humanity. They bring healing messages of love, forgiveness, and unity through their hands. They bring peace and harmony through words, music, or art. The fourth-plane Lightworkers are the artists whose glorious works beatify the Earth plane, the composers who give us music to lift and enlighten our spirits, and the writers and poets who change the world with their words. All works of art, literature, music, and objects of beauty come from this plane.

Lightworkers from the fourth plane can:

- Have strong compassion for others.
- Be very empathic toward others.
- Have strong creative abilities.
- Be prolific writers.
- Have musical talents.
- Have an eye for beauty.
- Have artistic abilities.
- Have powerful healing capabilities.

Lightworkers from the fourth plane make excellent poets, authors, composers, singers, designers, architects, and energy healers.

### Fourth-plane Lightworker facts:

*Color:* green

*Element:* air

*Sensitive body parts:* heart, lungs, diaphragm, chest, thymus, circulatory system, shoulders, arms, hands

*Basic strengths:* love, compassion, kindness, forgiveness, hope, sympathy, empathy

*Gemstones and crystals:* emerald

*Flower essences:* bleeding heart, holly, wild rose

*Essential oils that soothe:* marjoram, rose

*Balancing foods:* green vegetables (such as broccoli, green beans, lettuce, Brussels sprouts)

### Famous fourth-plane Lightworkers:

Vincent Van Gogh, Ludwig van Beethoven, Shakespeare, Frank Lloyd Wright, John Lennon, Mother Teresa of Calcutta, Queen Elizabeth I.

## The Fifth Plane

"Be the change you wish to see in the world."

—Mahatma Gandhi

The fifth plane is a realm of illumination. This is the place where all the wisdom of creation is stored and where all knowledge is accessed. The cures for diseases are developed here; technology that will revolutionize life on Earth is invented here. All scientific discoveries come to humanity through beings from the fifth plane. Information on spiritual enlightenment comes to Earth from here as well. All the answers to the mysteries of the universe can be discovered in the fifth plane. Knowledge to enlighten humanity in all areas is stored here.

Lightworkers from the fifth plane can:

- Be powerful visionaries.
- Have strong clairvoyant abilities.
- Hhave the ability to enlighten the masses.
- Be ahead of their time.
- Have prolific dreams.
- Have a powerful imagination.
- Have strong telepathic capabilities.
- Have superior intellectual capabilities.
- Be people who can change the world.

Lightworkers from the fifth plane make excellent scientists, metaphysicians, spiritual gurus, world leaders, medical researchers, inventers, philosophers, creators of advanced technology, and prophets.

### Fifth-plane Lightworker facts:

*Color*: blue

*Element*: ether

*Sensitive body parts*: throat, neck, ears, jaw, mouth, teeth, gums, tongue, thyroid gland

*Basic strengths*: communication, creativity, expression, humility, manifesting ideas

*Gemstones and crystals*: sapphire, blue topaz, turquoise

*Flower essences*: lotus, buttercup, larch

*Essential oils that soothe*: chamomile, orange, rosemary

*Balancing foods*: fruits (such as blueberries, blackberries)

### Famous fifth-plane Lightworkers

Albert Einstein, Jonas Salk, Plato, Socrates, Mahatma Gandhi, Thomas Edison, Nostradamus, Edgar Cayce, Deepak Chopra.

## The sixth plane

"All truth passes through three stages: first, it is ridiculed; next it is violently attacked; finally, it is held to be self-evident."

—Arthur Schopenhauer

Ascended masters and archangels belong in the sixth plane. This realm is reserved for those of only the highest frequency—just before Source. These spiritually enlightened beings were once mere mortals and now, near completion of their spiritual evolution, have limitless powers. This type of Lightworker descends to Earth to serve humanity when there is to be a major shift in consciousness or a time of great enlightenment and healing. Ascended masters serve as the teachers of mankind and encompass gifts from all the realms. They also come and go at will from the Earth plane without experiencing birth or death. Human evolution is overseen from this plane.

Lightworkers from the sixth plane can:

- Serve as teachers for humanity.
- Create a shift in consciousness.
- Appear on Earth, forgoing the birth and death process.
- Create increased spiritual awareness.
- Heal the planet's energy.
- Assist with the expansion of light energy.
- Oversee human evolution.

Lightworkers from the sixth plane make great spiritual leaders, guardian angels, and healers, although they need no material possessions and could take pretty much any form—not necessarily a high-profile one. No occupation, title, or moniker could ever begin to describe the wisdom and experience of these light beings. Such a Lightworker could even appear as a bum on the street! Their light energy will draw those in need of spiritual enlightenment toward them automatically.

**Sixth-plane Lightworker facts:**

*Color:* indigo

*Element:* light

*Sensitive body parts:* brain, eyes, lymphatic and endocrine systems

*Basic strengths:* clairvoyance, telepathy, wisdom, connection to the higher self

*Gemstones and crystals:* amethyst, azurite, indigo

*Flower essences:* lavender, sunflower

*Essential oils that soothe:* sage, lavender, lemon

*Balancing foods:* dark fruits (such as blueberries, blackberries, red grapes)

### Famous sixth-plane Lightworkers

Jesus Christ, Buddha, Saint Michael the Archangel, the Blessed Virgin Mother Mary, Muhammad.

## The Seventh Plane

"So powerful is the light of unity that it can illuminate the whole world."—Baha'u'llah

This is where Source exists—our Creator. It is all that is. Without it, nothing would exist. When a spirit finally reunites with Source, it has completed its spiritual journey. In this realm, each spirit retains its individuality while also becoming one with the Almighty. Source, as described previously, is an ever-expanding and evolving energy force. The spirits who ascend to this level have achieved the highest amount of light and add to the infinity experience within Source. This is where God is. Lightworkers from the seventh plane become part of Source Energy, which:

* Is our Creator.
* Is composed of energy.
* Is all-knowing.
* Is what connects all life force in the universe.
* Knows only unconditional love.
* Has no concept of time.
* Is eternal.

**Seventh-plane Lightworker facts:**

*Color:* white

*Element:* energy

*Sensitive body parts:* center of the head, fontanel

*Basic strengths:* wisdom, absolute knowing, unconditional love, universal higher consciousness

*Gemstones and crystals:* diamond, black opal

*Flower essences:* lotus, star tulip

*Essential oils that strengthen connection:* geranium, sandalwood

*Balancing foods:* water, fasting

As you read over the descriptions of each plane, one will resonate deeply with you. Are you the person who always seeks to help others? Are you creatively gifted in any way? Do you wish to bring illumination to the Earth plane by working in a spiritual practice? When you identify which plane you have descended from, use the Lightworker facts associated with that plane to support you in your day-to-day existence. Wear the listed color, carry the suggested crystal or gemstone, and meditate while the scent of the recommended flower essence drifts through the air. Realizing your true self and your life purpose will permit you to feel connected to who you really are and will allow you the freedom to live in the loving space that you were meant to be in.

# Part II:

# Sacred Gifts From Source

4

# Psychic: Lifting the Veil

When we hear the word *psychic*, it conjures up all kinds of mysterious images, including turbans, crystal balls, and gypsies in a caravan. Yes, there is real history behind these images, but I think it's time to take some of the mystery out of the mystical. The first step is to understand that everyone is born psychic, although most people are at a loss when it comes to understanding or using this remarkable ability. Let's examine the inherent qualities that we are each born with that make us psychic. Lightworkers or not, we are all born with some degree of these attributes, which have five main components:

1. Sensitivity (an awareness of our five senses).
2. Intuition (feelings of knowing without any concrete information).
3. Awareness (cognition or alertness to our surroundings).
4. Empathy (experiencing emotions or feelings that match another person's).
5. Belief (the absolute knowing of things unseen).

There's really nothing mystical about these five attributes. It's easy to understand how we all have them and use them on a daily basis. Some of us use one or more of these components more than others and some of us have higher intensities of one component more than the others. But the bottom line is that these five components and their level of intensity are what make up our psychic abilities. Because we are each different, we each need to discover our own psychic strengths. In this section of the book, we will look at these five components in detail so you can discover which ones you possess in higher intensities. This understanding will help you develop your unique gifts.

## The Lightworker's Heightened Components

Being extremely sensitive creatures, Lightworkers have heightened intensities of all five components. While this is certainly a gift they bring to the world, it feels more like a curse to the unaware Lightworker. In fact, these five components in heightened intensities can bring much disruption to the Lightworker's personal life. It is like turning the volume all the way up on your headphones and trying to go about your day-to-day life with music constantly blasting in your ears. If you don't know where the volume control is, the overload can bring on meltdowns and cause great stress. Being super-sensitive can create anxiety, and the powerful empathy a Lightworker experiences towards the collective consciousness can bring on severe depression. In addition, intuitive messages often come via physical symptoms (what we call gut instincts), which can create illnesses.

These heightened intensities can cause an avalanche of emotions and feelings that seemingly come out of nowhere. This is why is it so important for Lightworkers to understand what they are experiencing and learn how to handle it. It is only natural that a Lightworker would want to soothe this unpleasantness and search out a variety of methods to quell these feelings. Some unaware Lightworkers may try to numb themselves with drugs and alcohol, some repeatedly get into destructive relationships, and others may turn their pain inward and try to harm themselves. Some Lightworkers totally shut down and withdraw from life altogether. But these choices create a vicious cycle. It is in Lightworkers' nature to be of service and to bring light to the world. When they are not fulfilling their divine mission, they experience even more feelings of worthlessness that just compound this unpleasant experience.

When Lightworkers do not know how to use their heightened components, they feel lost. As we explore each of these five components in separate chapters, we will discuss healthier and more productive ways to combat the challenging effects of these extra-sensory perceptions. We'll also discuss how Lightworkers can learn to use these abilities to serve humanity.

Although not all mental illnesses or conditions are a result of being an unaware Lightworker, many Lightworkers can indeed find relief with the realization of their true identity and purpose. Even though this is profoundly helpful, it doesn't mean a Lightworker's challenges are over. His or her place on Earth is not an easy space to inhabit. Because Lightworkers tend to absorb the feelings of others around them, they may often feel excessively drained or exhausted. At times, Lightworkers may feel overwhelmed with the awesome task they have agreed to take on before they ever came to Earth. They take on the weight of humanity and then find it difficult to cast light in a world that is cloaked in darkness. Lightworkers who do not know how to manage heightened components may suffer:

- Depression.
- Anxiety.
- Addictions.
- Mood swings.
- Sudden waves of sadness.
- Psychosomatic illness.
- Feelings of worthlessness.
- Low self-esteem.
- Antisocial behavior.
- Feelings of isolation.
- Repeatedly getting into dysfunctional relationships.
- Impulses to commit self-harm (such as cutting the flesh or pulling out hair).

## Learning to Shield Yourself

To avoid as many of these challenges as possible, Lightworkers require ongoing cleansing and shielding. A woman named Marcy whom I met at a spiritual circle learned this the hard way. Marcy was a budding intuitive who was learning to develop her psychic abilities. Each week as the class began, we would open the circle with a meditation. I noticed many times Marcy would get up and leave the room in the middle of the meditation. When the teacher finally asked Marcy if she was all right, Marcy replied that she began to feel "uncomfortable" during the meditations and needed to stop. The teacher offered her some grounding techniques and Marcy agreed to give them a try and thanked her.

As the weeks went on, Marcy and I became friendly and we started to go out for a cup of coffee together after class. We talked about how we loved the class, exploring spirituality, and studying metaphysics. Marcy told me she wanted to hone her skills so she could work with the public and actually help people with her gifts some day. But then Marcy began to attend less and less, and finally, she stopped coming all together. I missed her and decided one day to give her a call. Marcy was happy to hear from me, but she explained that she dropped out of class because she was not "meant to do this." I told her I didn't understand why she felt that way because she had been doing wonderfully with her readings and had often talked about how much she loved the class. Marcy went on to explain that each week during the guided mediations, she would begin to feel uncomfortable, frigid, and even sick to her stomach. Sometimes she would get flashes of frightening images, such as explosions, faces of people in horrific pain, and chaotic scenes that were so traumatic that she needed to stop the meditation and get out of the room. These experiences scared Marcy, and she felt drained for days after each class. It had gotten so bad that it interfered with her job.

I explained to Marcy that during meditation, she was inadvertently opening up and absorbing energies that were not her own. I also explained that although this had been extremely unpleasant, it was also a good indication that her psychic components were heightened and intense enough to enable her to work with the public one day. But at the moment, with her limited training, Marcy hadn't learned how to handle this. And the collective energy of everyone in the class had just compounded the effect.

Marcy never realized how sensitive she was and what the effects of opening up to receiving energies in a conscious way could feel like. We discussed ways to guard against this in the future, and just being aware of this helped her feel better. With some practice, she was able to return to the class, where she practiced ways to separate and block energies that were outside her own energy field. (We will explore exactly how to do this in Chapter 5.)

I also suggested that the class facilitator cleanse and bless the room after each session because residual dark energy can affect sensitive individuals who come into such a space later on. It was an excellent learning experience for all of us!

## Taking It to the Limit

Sometimes feeling the effects of these heightened components goes even further. Some Lightworkers repeatedly experience certain extraordinary events in their lives that can confuse, upset, and even traumatize them if they don't recognize these experiences for what they are—the very normal result of their extremely acute nature. Although these events are certainly not exclusive to Lightworkers, if you have experienced one or more of them, I urge you to read this part of the book carefully and explore the possibility that you are indeed a Lightworker. Some of these experiences include:

- Having prophetic dreams.
- Having premonitions of worldwide disasters.
- Feeling disconnected from your body.
- Experiencing (and eventually overcoming) addictions.
- Being prone to anxiety.
- Suffering unexplained bouts of depression.
- Having irrational fears.
- Having an overactive central nervous system.
- Experiencing adverse effects of medications.
- Experiencing ringing in your ears or other hearing disturbances.
- Having out-of-body experiences.
- Having a near-death experience.
- Being present when loved ones cross over.
- Seeing or communicating with the deceased.

The next five chapters will look at each of the components we are all born with that make us psychic. As you read these chapters and discover where your own intensities are, you will begin to see them as gifts instead of hindrances. You'll also get some solid guidance on how to use these five components as tools that will both enhance your life and help balance the energy of the planet.

# 5

# Sensitivity: Stimulation Overload

Are there days when you feel like you could just jump out of your skin? Do you sometimes feel a sudden rush of anxiety that seems to come out of nowhere? We are all born with some level of sensitivity, and some of us are more sensitive than others. But the kind of sensitivity this chapter will discuss is more than merely being emotional enough to cry at greeting card commercials.

Our five senses—sight, sound, touch, smell, and taste—are meant to give our physical bodies the tools we need to maneuver in the physical world. But in Lightworkers, one or more of these senses can be so acute that they tend to go beyond the physical and extend out into the ethers to connect with Source Energy.

This can make them hypersensitive to outside stimulation, such as noise, light, or even other people, and they may have strong reactions to these stimuli even when the stimuli don't seem to bother anyone else around them.

This sensory overload can cause Lightworkers not only physical but also emotional stress—especially when a Lightworker is not aware of why he or she is so sensitive and has no idea what to do about it. As a child, I suffered from anxiety attacks that persisted until I understood the true nature of my Lightworker soul and why I was feeling the anxiety. Only with this realization can Lightworkers appreciate their hypersensitivities as the gifts they are and learn to manage and develop them into psychic abilities that will guide their lives here on Earth.

## What's Your Sensitivity?

If I hear a loud noise, I will feel it deeply in my bones. If I'm in a room with too much sunlight streaming in, I won't sit by the window because I will actually feel pain. I'm constantly dimming the lights in my house. I am also highly sensitive to temperature and always feel cold. I have so many sensitivities that I have had to alter my lifestyle to cope with them all. What situations make you feel overwhelmed? Make a list of any physical symptoms you have on a regular basis when exposed to various stimuli in the outside world. To help you make your list, think about the following questions:

* How do you respond to loud music?
* Will a loud noise make you jump?
* Does someone standing too close to you make you jump out of your skin?

- Does light really hurt your eyes?
- Do certain materials, such as wool, really annoy you?
- Do other people tell you that you're too sensitive?
- Does caffeine make you bounce off the walls more than most people?
- Do you panic in crowds?
- When someone walks into a room, do you feel a shift in your own mood?
- Do you dislike perfume or does cologne give you a headache?
- Do you suffer from food allergies or sensitivities?
- Do certain over-the-counter cold medications give you adverse reactions or have the opposite effect from what the bottle indicates?

There are no right or wrong answers to these questions, of course. But examining those questions you answered with a *yes* will give you an indication of where your Lightworker sensitivities are strongest and where you should focus you attention.

## What Does Your Sensitivity Mean?

Because we all have different sensitivities and different degrees of sensitivity, some of us are more likely to be able to interpret energies with one of our five senses than we are with the others. Analyzing your sensitivities will give you a good idea of how to use your Lightworker abilities and what area (or areas) of Lightwork you can excel in.

For example, if you are sensitive to noise, you will be a Lightworker who hears messages from the spirit world, because your sense of hearing is heightened. If you are sensitive to certain materials against your skin, you could be a Lightworker with hands-on healing skills who excels in therapeutic touch. If you are sensitive to bright lights or have strong reactions to images, you will be a Lightworker who receives messages from your spirit guides and teachers by seeing pictures. The following heightened senses go along with various extra-sensory abilities:

- Sensitivity to sight: clairvoyant (clear sight).
- Sensitivity to noise: clairaudient (clear hearing).
- Sensitivity to pain or touch: clairsentient (clear feeling).
- Sensitivity to smell: clairalient (clear smell).
- Sensitivity to feeling: claircognizant (clear knowing).

Although the following spiritual practices could incorporate all your senses, here are a few suggestions of practices you might expect to excel at, depending on your type of sensitivity:

- Heightened sensitivity to sight: aura reading, tarot or oracle card reading, remote viewing, mediumship, spirit art.
- Heightened sensitivity to sound: mediumship, spirit rescue, sound healing, working with electronic voice phenomenon (EVP).
- Heightened sensitivity to touch: energy healing (including Reiki), psychometry, working as an intuitive advisor.
- Heightened sensitivity to smell: mediumship, aromatherapies, candle therapy.

* Heightened sensitivity to taste: mediumship, holistic healing, herbal remedies.

## Signs of Things to Come

Lightworkers may also get precognitive sensitivities. If I sense something is about to happen, for example, I will get very pronounced goosebumps. (Some of my colleagues who also experience this call them "spiritbumps" and take them as a sign of validation for their psychic messages or validations.) This type of reaction aligns with your sense of touch or feeling; your skin is literally reacting to the awareness that something is about to occur. Heightened hearing can work this way, as well. For example, right before my mother calls me, I will usually hear a ringing in my ears. Most times, within five minutes, the phone will ring and it will be her. Pay special attention to the way you were feeling before something big happened. Did you feel anxious in the days before a major earthquake? Did you feel light and happy for no apparent reason right before your boss surprised you with a large bonus? These emotional or physical symptoms may be precognition. By paying attention to your own signals, you will learn your personal signs of things to come.

## Ways to Prevent Short-Circuiting

As I mentioned in the beginning of this chapter, excess stimulation can cause physical and emotional stress. Because heightened sensitivity effects all five senses, symptoms can include any number of symptoms, such as:

* Anxiety.
* Nervousness.
* Unwarranted or irrational fears.
* Restlessness.
* Headaches.
* Dizziness.
* Chronic pain (due to conditions such as fibromyalgia or restless leg syndrome).
* Feelings of being detached from your body.

Unaware Lightworkers may seek to medicate themselves to quell the uncomfortable feelings their sensitivities bring on. This can create addiction issues or worse yet, totally block out their powerful Lightworker gifts, which then begins a cycle of feeling lost, misplaced, and worthless. Fortunately, you can rely on much better ways to relieve yourself of the unpleasant feelings associated with being hypersensitive.

Awareness of what your sensitivities mean and being able to see them as the gifts they are, are the firsts step in learning to deal with them. For example, when I was eight years old, my mother wasn't feeling well one week, and soon after, I suffered my first anxiety attack. My sensitivities to someone who was sick brought on the anxiety. Although as I mentioned, I suffered with anxiety attacks and irrational fears for many years, this stopped happening once I became more tuned-in to my own sensitivities and my identity as a Lightworker. Making lifestyle adjustments to eliminate or limit your triggers also helps. That includes learning what foods, drinks, or even medications may set you off. If I have caffeine any time during the day, then I'm up all night. And I simply cannot take any over-the-counter medication that contains diphenhydramine (the antihistamine used in Benadryl) because it keeps me up for hours with nervous jitters—even though this drug makes most people sleepy. Certain environments may also set you off, necessitating that you either avoid the place entirely, if you can, or that you learn to shield yourself. Perhaps your house harbors energy that you are sensitive to because of events that occurred there in the past or people who have lived there before—like the old house my friend David bought. David didn't need to move out, but he did need help getting rid of the troubled spirit hanging around his house.

Major electrical lines are another example of how your environment can throw your system off balance, particularly if you are clairsentient (sensitive to feel or touch). This happened to a friend's young daughter who attended a summer day camp located on a campus bisected by a string of huge electrical towers. My friend's normally mild-mannered child, who had no problems going to school the rest of the year, cried and cried when dropped off at camp—despite the fact that her best friend also attended the camp and that the program included many activities that the little girl loved. The counselors tried to work with the girl, but day after day, they ended up calling her mother to come pick up the child. After just a week, my friend pulled her daughter from that day camp and sent her to one in a different location, where she was fine.

You may also find that certain people, because of the dark energy they harbor, can also act as triggers for you. This is true not only for people who upset or annoy you, but also for people who are depressed. Remember that your reactions come not from whether you like these people, but from how their energy interacts with yours. This is why learning how to shield yourself is invaluable.

Below is a list of general lifestyle tips that you may find useful in preventing stimulation overload:

* Engage in a daily exercise routine.
* Drink plenty of water.
* Avoid caffeine.
* Avoid over-the-counter medication containing high levels of diphenhydramine.
* Keep your personal environment as organized as possible.
* Remove any old or outdated items from your space that may harbor old energies.
* Retreat into a quiet, dark space to center yourself.
* Avoid crowds whenever possible.
* Feel gratitude for how your gifts of hypersensitivity can serve others.
* Shield yourself when necessary.

## A Word About Sensitive Children

While some babies sleep the night away, content as can be, others are cranky and fussy, experiencing what doctors call colic. Some even have food sensitivities or allergies to certain materials. Could the fussy, colicky baby be more sensitive? Most likely, the answer is yes.

These babies may cry a lot, have trouble sleeping, and need to be comforted more often than most because they are highly sensitive to the energies and vibrations around them. These children are likely to develop extra-sensory perceptions much more easily than those who don't seem to be fazed by much. Recently, we have seen an increase of children who have sensitivity issues. Many are classified as having "special needs," and sadly, a large number of them are medicated.

Because the Earth plane is currently heavy with dark energy, increasing numbers of these sensitive Lightworkers will incarnate to help balance the energy of the planet. The fact that we are seeing an increase in the numbers of these types of children tells us that these energetic shifts are indeed occurring.

Here are some possible indicators that your child may have heightened senses. He or she:

- Is easily startled.
- May not always sleep soundly.
- Cries easily.
- May have food allergies.
- Dislikes wearing clothing.
- Has strong reactions (like or dislike) to strangers.
- Is sensitive to noises.
- becomes anxious in crowds.
- Is very sensitive to temperature (especially in food or a bottle).
- Reacts strongly to smells.
- Has an unusual amount of unwarranted fears.

As a child, I was extremely emotional, fearful, and anxious due to my heightened sensitivity. I had a tremendous amount of difficulty in school. Both the learning disability I was diagnosed with (dyslexia, which is actually a gift) and my sensitive nature made it nearly impossible for me to focus on my schoolwork. I was reacting to the highly charged, chaotic energy of a busy classroom full of children.

My teachers labeled me lazy and impatient because I would rush through my work, getting it all wrong, just so I could have some time to space out, instinctively going into the ether to shield myself from the energies that were tormenting me. (A sensitive child can easily become ungrounded and disconnected from the Earth plane just to cope.) My teachers' negative assessment of me and the way they then treated me caused me to have strong feelings of worthlessness and low self-esteem.

I often wonder how much more positive my school years would have been if an adult had recognized this and helped me with some shielding exercises. If you have a child who is easily distracted or who is experiencing problems focusing on schoolwork, he or she could be hypersensitive and having a reaction to the energies bombarding him or her. Allowing such a child to decompress with some down time at the end of the school day can be very helpful. Depending on your child's personality, this down time could include talking a walk in the park; reading him or her a calming story; taking a nice, relaxing bath (water will dilute and wash away a lot of the excess energies), or even just having some quiet time.

Such children need this time after school to shake off the energies they have been exposed to all day long in the classroom. Avoid rushing this type of hypersensitive child to another activity (such as a team sport, music lesson, or club), allowing the child to watch television or play video games immediately after school, or pushing the child to jump right into homework. You may also find it helpful to eliminate caffeinated drinks (including soda) and foods with excess sugars from their diet. A calm, secure, and loving home environment is a must for sensitive Lightworker children. By practicing some of the methods discussed here, you will be giving them a head start in learning to cope with their sensitivities.

## Learning How to Shield Yourself

Shielding is a vital technique you should practice daily—not only when you sense you need it. (Think of it as an important prevention tool, like taking vitamins or brushing your teeth.) Shielding not only keeps you grounded, but also prevents your energy field from absorbing the negative energies around you.

You can use a variety of techniques to shield yourself, but start with this relatively simple exercise. Later, you can change or adapt it, if you'd like.

1. Picture yourself inside a bubble with a white light from your Higher Power above your head.

2. Envision this white light encircling your entire body, including the bottom of your feet.

3. Tell yourself that this bubble of light shields you from all of life's anxieties, as well as troubles and dangers.

4. Allow yourself to feel the strength of this protective white light, which is so strong that nothing can penetrate it—so nothing negative can touch you.

When you then encounter troubles as you go about your day, simply remember your protective bubble and the light-inducing emotions it engenders. This works well when you're in a crowd of people and feel surrounded by negative energy, as well as if you're in a conflict at home or work. Anytime you go to a party or other large gathering with lots of people and lots of stimulation, remember to shield yourself first. Shielding yourself before you get into a car (whether you're driving or just a passenger) is also a good practice.

## Taking on Other People's Energy

It's now time to take a deeper look at being sensitive to energy fields other than your own. (This is different from empathy, which we will discuss in a later chapter.) Perhaps you're in a great mood, and then your friend calls. He's all doom and gloom. He talks about how his stocks are taking a dive and how he'll never sell his house. He doesn't think he can pay for college for his kids anymore. Even though you know he's just worried and that everything will probably work out just fine, suddenly your good mood is out the window. Out of the blue, you experience a major headache. Or maybe you come home from the gym feeling totally energized from your workout, only to find your roommate feeling sluggish, sitting like a lump on the couch in a depressed mood. Suddenly, you feel incredibly tired, even though just a minute ago, you felt amazing.

What's going on here? If you're sensitive to other people, then it's very easy for you to absorb their energy and think that it's your own energy, and the adverse reactions will manifest through one of your five heightened senses. The key here is to stop the momentum of the dark energies and recognize what is happening, distinguish and separate which energy is yours and which belongs to the other person, and then shield yourself.

If your husband or wife walks in after having a bad day at the office, you can certainly commiserate with your spouse, but also be sure to distinguish his or her energy from your own by simply separating the two in your mind. Your job isn't to live someone else's energy.

Highly sensitive people would also do well to avoid violent TV shows or movies, because it's possible to absorb the negative feelings just from watching them unfold on the screen. Suddenly, you go from having a calm demeanor to screaming at the kids. This isn't limited to horror movies—even watching talk shows or reading about someone's tragic life in the paper or tabloids without shielding yourself first can cause you to experience disturbances for days afterwards. Paying attention to how you react in these situations is important.

Do you experience changes in your body (achiness or overall tiredness) or in your mood (depression or feeling edgy)? Or do you begin to have disturbing and vivid dreams or thoughts?

Again, be conscious not to allow energies that are not your own to take over your senses. It's hard today to remain positive when you flip on the news and watch the dismal economic reports, so consider limiting the amount of TV news you watch and avoid filling your head with the unnecessary clutter of daytime talk shows or soap operas.

## Taking on the Weight of the World

A Lightworkers' senses are highly affected by the collective consciousness. As the universal energy shifts with major occurrences on the planet, so will your heightened senses. That is tough to combat, but you can get through it. When tragic events occur on our planet, the Lightworkers will often feel the effects. Even on the anniversary of 9/11, for example, I'll feel a total depression sweeping over me, or I may begin seeing disturbing visions during my meditations. It's very important to remain aware of what is happening in the world so you can connect how you are feeling to current events for later reference. Did you suffer a panic attack before the tsunami in Thailand in December 2004 or the Haitian earthquake in January 2010? Were you feeling sad the week before Michael Jackson and Farrah Fawcett passed away? Did you hear a ringing in your ears right before a major plane crash was reported on the news?

Every time an event occurs that affects the collective energy of the Earth plane, you may experience some strange sensory reactions to it that are totally unrelated to what is happening in your own life. It's important to note these correlations, because this knowledge will help you to cope with your feelings at the time and also to process them more quickly in the future. It will also help you to predict events to come by knowing your reactionary symptoms.

When you feel these effects of the collective energy, pull yourself out by connecting with the beauty of our planet. Go on a walk in nature and breathe in some fresh air to balance your vibrational equilibrium. Connecting with trees or to anything with roots that are planted firmly in the Earth will help ground your energy. Hugging a tree or laying on top of a large rock will immediately ground you and connect you with the light energy available on the Earth plane.

Sensitivity is just one aspect of being a Lightworker. As your heightened five senses go beyond your physical body (which sometimes has a challenge controlling them), remember that the sensitive nature of your spirit is a gift meant to help you heal the planet. Learning to use these gifts in a productive way will not only help you, but it will give you the opportunity to help others.

Next, we will examine the second attribute of all Lightworkers—intuition.

# 6

# Intuition: Accessing the Ethereal Hard Drive

Let's begin with the meaning of the word *intuition* itself: the act or faculty of knowing or sensing without the use of rational processes; immediate cognition. People who are intuitive have inexplicable gut feelings that often turn out to be correct. This isn't actually all that surprising when you remember that even though we are each encased in a physical body, we are all also made up of energy and connected by Source. Our physical body needs the five physical senses to guide us through the world, but our energetic body is directly connected to an all-knowing Source and can go beyond the constraints of the physical world. Intuition is the very natural result of our energetic selves connecting with Source and accessing information that our physical senses cannot perceive. And because we are all a part of Source, we all have intuitive feelings. Every one of us has experienced intuition at one time or another. If you ever knew who was on the phone before you answered it or just had a funny feeling that you should not turn down a certain street, you have accessed information that comes from beyond the physical world.

When you spontaneously access this information from Source, also referred to as Source intelligence, you are unknowingly accessing an infinite knowledge pool that is available to every living creature on the planet. Even animals share in Source's intelligence because they, too, are part of Source Energy. It's no accident when a family pet travels hundreds of miles to find the family that left it behind. These animals simply access Source intelligence, which most people would simply call instinct. Think of how a baby develops in the womb, how cells continue to multiply over and over until a new person is formed. Consider how intricately and precisely designed a flower is, with each petal perfectly placed, or how the sun rises and sets each day. Many complex and beautiful things in our world that we take for granted do not exist the way they do by mere chance. They are perfectly planned by our Creator's intelligence—Source intelligence. Think of it as a giant computer with a non-corruptible hard drive that stores information about everything that ever is, was, or shall be.

Psychics are tapping into Source intelligence when they access information for their clients about future events. I chuckle whenever I hear psychics say they don't know where their information comes from, or when one of them says, "Spirit is telling me..." Spirit, some powerful, all-knowing being in the sky, gets all the credit (or blame) for the information the psychic is giving his or her client. But what the psychic is actually doing is akin to logging into a giant computer, accessing the hard drive of Source's intelligence, and extracting information.

## Why Some Psychics Are Wrong

If all Source knowledge is pure and true, then why are some psychics inaccurate? All information from Source *is* pure and true—it's the translation that psychics sometimes get wrong. The size of the psychic's ego usually determines the accuracy of the intuitive information the psychic relays. If the psychic cannot put his or her own personal opinions, feelings, and prejudices in proper perspective, the information will be distorted. Think of the psychic as a filter or channel for information to funnel through. The channel must be clear if the information is to remain pure. If the filter or channel gets muddied, miscommunication results. It works much like the children's game Telephone or Whisper Down the Lane—by the time the original message reaches the last person in line, it's usually unrecognizable.

## Intuition for Lightworkers

Lightworkers are acutely (and sometimes painfully) intuitive. But just like everyone else, they must combat the ego. If they filter out intuitive information based solely on their own ego-driven frames of reference, experiences, or desires, then the amount of information they are willing to accept will be limited. And even worse, a Lightworker can be literally tortured by intuitive feelings he or she does not act upon. By working hard at putting the ego aside, on the other hand, Lightworkers automatically become open to all possibilities and all outcomes, which allows intuitive information to come easier. Lightworkers will naturally use this intensified intuition to help others find their way, causing those others to be drawn to the Lightworkers and depend on them for guidance. This makes Lightworkers perfect for any service profession. Lightworkers who recognize, accept, and trust their intuition to be their guide when making major life choices are also natural manifesters.

## Establishing a Sense of Trust

If you are to develop and use your intuition as a Lightworker, it is vital that you recognize what is happening when ego tries to step in and say, "You're just being paranoid," or 'That could never happen!" Believe me, the truth is that it most probably *will* happen! Because the ego is composed of pure fear, it will *never* trust Source. It actually trusts no one. Circumventing ego to establish an absolute trust in Source may sound impossible, but I assure you that for a Lightworker, it's not. Remind yourself of your place in the collective. We are each like drops of water in an ocean; no matter how small, each drop is guided by the tide. If we trust that the tide is always going in the right direction, it's easier to go with the flow. Focusing on the connectedness we all share through Source and the loving feeling this brings us instead of focusing on our ego-driven fear is the key. Many of my clients come to me already knowing the answers they seek; they are simply looking for validation or confirmation of what they already know.

When you disregard the information that you get intuitively because you don't trust it or need someone else to validate it for you, then you can't make the best choices and you can't help others as effectively. A good example is a story my husband told me about a detective who didn't listen to his gut when he was assigned the case of a missing boy. Two weeks after he was reported missing, the boy had been found dead near a riverbank in an apparent drowning accident. The boy's stepfather told the police that the 12-year-old had played many times near the riverbank and that he had warned the boy that one day he could slip and fall in. After hours of interviewing the stepfather, the detective found no evidence of any foul play. Yet something just felt "off." The detective could sense that the stepfather was hiding something, even though all the facts seemed to point to an accidental drowning. Weeks later, the boy's autopsy reported that his cause of death was not drowning at all—it was strangulation. It then came out that the stepfather had a history of domestic violence. By that time, the stepfather had left the state, and to this day he is still at large. If the detective had acted on his instincts, he could have found some reason to detain the man. But he doubted himself and instead let the murderer go free. Source gave him the right information, but not wanting to make a mistake in detaining the stepfather, the detective had more fear than trust in his gut feelings.

## Intuition Already Guides You

Many of us operate on intuitive feelings more often than we realize. Intuition guides us in all areas of our lives, bringing us opportunities and keeping us safe, even if we may not pay much attention to these subtle insights. But paying closer attention to them so we recognize them for what they are can pay off. I know a man who was about to get on a plane from Los Angeles to New York. He was a frequent business traveler and his life was basically spent in airports. One night when it was clear and starry outside, he had a nagging feeling while he waited at his gate. "I just felt like I shouldn't get on that plane," he told me. The flight was sold out and the plane was leaving exactly on time. There was no real reason for this man to miss his flight home, but he just kept having that strange but persistent feeling that he should stay put and go the following morning—even though that would mean having to reschedule an important breakfast meeting the next morning. The man walked up to the counter and changed his flight to go the next day because he always listened to that little voice inside of him. Why not? It never steered him wrong.

Later that night at a hotel, he received a call saying his mother, who lived in Los Angeles, had just had a mild heart attack. If he had taken that flight, it would have taken this man two days to get back from across the country due to winter storms and airport delays. But for reasons he couldn't explain, he was still in Los Angeles. and was able to get to the hospital relatively quickly. His mother was in intensive care, but she pulled through risky heart surgery. Was it because her beloved son was at her side? Would she have made it through the night without him? No one can really say. What I do know is that this man made exactly the right decision. He trusted that little voice inside of him that told him that there was a problem with him getting on that flight.

## Recognizing Intuition

The first step to developing your intuitive powers is to recognize them. You must accept the fact that you are intuitive and see your hunches as real messages instead of writing them off because they sound crazy. Mary learned this when her 7-year-old daughter Bree came home from school with an invitation to spend a weekend camping with a classmate, her mother, and several other friends to celebrate the classmate's birthday. Immediately, Mary had a bad feeling about it.

She didn't know the other girl's mother, and she worried if her daughter would be safe on the trails around the campground, which was also surrounded by very deep lakes. Even though she was afraid she was being too overprotective, Mary said no to the trip, and Bree cried for days. After the weekend, Mary found out that although the mother had tried hard to keep control of the 10 girls who came on the trip, one of them had been lost on the trails for more than two hours. Mary then realized that she hadn't just been an overprotective mom. She'd been listening to her intuition, which had kept her daughter safe.

Mark had a similar experience when he wanted to buy a house in suburban Atlanta. It was a cute little ranch that needed some work, but because Mark worked in construction, he knew he could fix it up. His bank approved the loan, and he looked at the property five times. But when he was preparing to make the offer, he had a strange feeling. Something was telling him not to buy that house, even though it seemed perfect for him. Mark didn't listen to his real estate agent, who was pressuring him to make the offer. "You'll lose the house," the agent told him. "So many families are waiting to make offers." Although Mark didn't understand why, he passed on the property. Three weeks later, his girlfriend of two years was offered her dream job in Florida. Mark thought about what his life would be like with him in Atlanta and his girlfriend in Florida. He proposed, and they just purchased their first house in Tampa.

Janet is a single mom who lives in Wisconsin with her 5-year-old son Nick. One snowy morning, Janet woke up with a horrible feeling in the pit of her stomach. Looking outside at the snow continuing to pile up, she couldn't pinpoint what was wrong. Then, when Nick wandered down the hall asking for waffles, she knew that for some reason she didn't want him getting on the school bus that morning. "It wasn't as if it was the snowiest day ever," she told me later. "We'd trudged off to the bus together in much worse weather before. But on that day, I kept hearing this strong voice inside me saying not to put Nick on that bus." This really put Janet in a jam, because her husband had already driven the SUV to work that morning and she didn't want to drive her son in their sports car during a snowstorm. "It sounded crazy," she said, "but I kept Nick home that day, promising myself that we would have an educational day and watch something on the Science Channel." Janet worried a little bit that her husband would think she was a crazy mother who didn't want to let her son take the necessary risks in life. But it didn't take long for Janet to find out that her little voice was right. Her local news channel soon reported that the school bus Nick usually took to school had skidded off the road and into a ditch at a place that was just two stops past Janet's house. Had she not listened to her intuition, Nick would have been on that bus. Hours later, more news reports came in that several of the children had been hospitalized. That night, Janet's husband held his wife closely and kept saying over and over again, "I won't ever call you crazy again." Little Nick even went to bed saying, "Thanks Mommy for not letting me crash today."

Many people have heard the amazing story about the 65-year-old cab driver from New York who sat outside the World Trade Center every single morning for 10 years. On

September 11, 2001, he had this nagging feeling that he needed to call his grown daughter in Chicago right away. He didn't own a cell phone, and his cab was way back in the line, so he left the cab for a moment to run around the corner and use a pay phone at a nearby gas station. He figured he'd just make a quick call and be right back. While he was on the pay phone, the first plane hit the World Trade Center. It wasn't long before his cab was under several feet of rubble. "I usually call my daughter on Sundays, but I just had a feeling I needed to call her. Nothing was wrong with her or my granddaughter," he marveled later. "It was like another force was out there, and it saved my life." The cab driver was certainly right in following his gut feeling, but it wasn't another force that was out there that saved him. It was his willingness to follow his inner knowing, a knowing that came from being connected to everything else "out there" in the universe.

I could go on and on telling similar stories of how grateful people were that they followed their intuition. And of course, using your intuition won't usually be quite so dramatic. The bottom line is that you will never, *ever* go wrong listening to your gut feelings. Even when it seems as if what you're getting doesn't make any sense, *recognize it as a message, and then listen to the message*. You might not understand it at the time, but you certainly will understand it later.

## How Much Do You Trust Your Intuition?

We all know someone who seems to get lucky breaks like this all the time. Like Forrest Gump, everything this person touches turns to gold. In fact, if we look at Forrest, we can see just how trusting he was. He never questioned his existence;

he just accepted it. "Life is like a box of chocolates," he said. "You never know what you're going to get." And that was that. We also all know people who seem to make awful choices all the time—those who perpetually suffer from "bum luck." These people have very little trust in their intuitive guidance and need to heighten their awareness. They also seem to have very little faith and are often suspicious or untrusting of others. They will say things like, "That's just my luck," as they hold onto limiting expectations of what their life should be like or of how they aren't as thin, rich, successful, or healthy as they would like to be. These people are getting intuitive information, just like the lucky ones, but instead of trusting their hunches, they doubt themselves—so their egos distort the knowledge that they get from Source.

How much do you trust your intuition? How many of the following things happen to you on at least a semi-regular basis?

- You drive in strange neighborhoods, but rarely get lost.
- Others tell you how lucky you are.
- You have prophetic dreams.
- You call a friend, only to hear him or her say, "I was just thinking of you!"
- You know who is calling before you answer the phone.
- After something bad happens, you can usually look back and see many signs of what was to come.
- You say to yourself or others, "I had a feeling..."

- You often turn on the radio or tune to a station just when a favorite song is playing.
- You know when someone is being untruthful.
- You think of someone, and soon after, you hear something about him or her.

If you were able to check off at least half of the items on this list, you probably trust your intuitive awareness and allow it to guide you. If you weren't able to claim that many, don't worry, it just means you have to work on your awareness and recognition of your own individual signals.

## Flexing Your Intuitive Muscle

In addition to getting intuitive feelings through emotional responses (such as when a situation just doesn't feel right or when you get a sudden urge to change your plans), intuition also comes in other ways. Some people get psychical signals, such as a headache, stomachache, or skin irritations (like the old saying about getting itchy palms meaning money is coming your way). You may even break out in hives! Your intuition will use many different ways to send you signals that something in your life is not what it seems to be. To become more aware of your intuitive feelings, however they come to you, practice the following:

- Remind yourself to trust in Source.
- Have an open mind.
- Be willing to take a chance.

* Maintain a calm, clear mentality that allows information to flow easily.

* Put your ego aside.

* Discard subjective information that casts doubt on Source information.

* Avoid having attachments to any particular outcome.

* Focus on and paying attention to subtle signs.

Remember, intuition isn't always (or even usually) like seeing a neon sign. Just a flash of a thought may cross your mind out of nowhere. Or you could suddenly get an odd emotional or physical sensation, however minor. This is how the intuitive process begins. The next time that happens, don't be too quick to discount it. After all, there is no tangible reason for intuitive feelings. They are not supposed to make sense. They aren't coming from our brains, being shaped by our logic and experience. Intuition goes way beyond the Earth plane and the limitation of our physical bodies. It is knowledge that comes from a higher place, from an infinite intelligence, that helps us bring more light into our lives and into the world.

# 7

# Awareness: Cosmic Consciousness

Stop and think of your day-to-day existence—how much of your day would you consider yourself to be on "auto pilot"? Because one of the components that make up your psychic abilities is awareness, it is important to be mindful of divine information that comes to you in the form of signs, signals, and synchronicities in your everyday life. These subtle (and sometimes not so subtle) messages come from the spirit world to get your attention. But if you don't recognize them, you'll miss the guidance.

Take Tina, for example. A CPA for a large accounting firm in Fort Lauderdale, she was not content with her life. Her job was mundane, her relationships never seemed to work out, and she had an overall feeling of emptiness inside. She yearned for a deeper meaning, a purpose in her life, because dealing with numbers, accounts, and money seemed so superficial. Every day, she would drive down a long highway to work, never noticing the 12-foot billboard that read, "Peace Corps, Inspiring Lives."

Guides are constantly sending signs and directions (and sometimes billboards) that most people choose to ignore. Even the more subtle signs will become visibly apparent as you raise your awareness. If you are reading this book, you already have raised your awareness enough to be curious and want to know more—so you're off to a good start.

What does it mean to raise your awareness level? It means opening your mind, accepting the possibility that there is more than what your physical eyes can see, and believing that you are always loved, supported, and have someone watching out for you. In order to benefit from all the information in this chapter, let's agree to be open to the idea that you are never alone.

## Spirit Guides

Spirit guides are Lightworkers from the third plane who choose to teach, support, and protect us. They are with us from the moment of our birth until we leave our physical bodies. Although our guides change as we grow and progress, we may have one or more working with us at any given time in the following aspects of our lives:

- Creative abilities.
- Spiritual progress.
- Work or business.

* Health, medical issues, or healing.

* Relationships.

Each guide has a particular expertise that fits with the different stages and phases of your life. For example, a kindergartener would not fare well in a college professor's classroom, just as you would not benefit from a guide or teacher from the spirit world who teaches higher-level lessons than you are not capable of absorbing at the time. Guides are given students who can benefit and learn from them, and as we master our life lessons and progress spiritually, our guides will change. Those who don't learn their lessons and instead spiritually stagnate might keep the same spirit guides for life. Many people ask me how they can distinguish their guide's voice from their own, and I tell them it's actually very easy. Your guide's voice is always loving and supportive, offering insight, words of caution, and gentle direction. It uplifts you and validates the choices you make.

When you hear a voice that tells you that you will never succeed or that you're not good enough, that's your ego talking. Your ego will always try to distract you from your goals with its insecurities and untrusting nature. Spirit guides are never critical, or degrading, or cause you to feel insecure. They will never tell you to harm yourself or others.

Being aware of the difference in these two voices will help you raise your awareness level and easily recognize when your guides are trying to communicate something to you.

## Becoming Aware of Your Spirit Guides

Many people describing their guides always seem to be talking about some Native American medicine man or an

Egyptian king. I find it funny how people never seem to mention having a spirit guide named Tony who owned a pizzeria in Newark, New Jersey, or maybe one who was a truck driver named Ralph. What good would an ordinary spirit guide do for us? The truth is that ordinary people have a lot to offer us, depending on the circumstances with which we are dealing.

To accommodate your comfort level, however, spirit guides will usually appear to you in a form you can identify with or relate to. So if you have a preconceived notion of what a guide should look like, your guide will do his best to conform to that expectation in order to establish a feeling of trust. This is not to fool or mislead you, because our guides no longer have physical bodies and so can choose to look any way they wish and still be sincere about it! The truth is, your spirit guide can appear in any form, as long as you believe that a being in that form might have something to teach you. The lessons guides come to teach can be anything, depending on your karma. Guides need not be highly evolved spirits who will channel the meaning of life through you. Your spirit guides are students on a soul's journey, just as you are. They have something to accomplish by guiding you, just as you have lessons to learn from them. Even if the guides assigned to us are not all-knowing, almighty beings, they *are* more advanced than their students.

Familiarize yourself with your guides as much as possible. Get to know them and learn their names. As you begin to recognize your guides' voices and know their personality traits, you will be allowed to glean more information about their true identity. You may find out, for example, that a spirit guide is a deceased loved one (maybe even someone you were named for), or perhaps even someone in your ancestry whose experience on Earth was similar to your own. These beings will have had experience in dealing with something that you are currently facing, so they can assist you in not making the same mistakes they made. At the same time, they may balance out some of their own karma by helping you, because these relationships are always reciprocal.

You may also have an animal for a spirit guide. In some cultures, people use animal guides or totems. This type of guide appears to be more of a companion than an actual teacher, although powerful energies, knowledge, and guidance can come from these creatures. Regardless of who acts as your guide, awareness of your guides' presence and the signs they give you in your everyday life will enhance your cognitive abilities.

## Getting Guidance From Angels

We should also be aware of messages coming from angels. My friend and colleague Eddie Mullins can certainly attest to that. One night when he was driving on an interstate, he heard an angel suddenly warning him to change lanes *now*. He did, and seconds later, a semi-truck entering the highway from an on-ramp turned over on its side, landing in the lane where Eddie had just been. After that encounter, Eddie began asking for everyday guidance, healing, and training from the angelic realm. He is now a gifted angel communicator, workshop leader, and a popular radio personality on SoulsJourneyRadio.com. Eddie explains more about these high-vibration beings:

> When we think of angels, beings of light and love sent directly from the Creator, we immediately feel warmth and unconditional love. The angels' main role is to deliver divine messages of love, peace, and harmony from the Creator. They are actually

the full extension of the Creator, and they are all around us to provide healing and to help us remember who we are so that we can live out our life's purpose while we are here on the Earth plane. Angels are ego-less and nondenominational and love all beings.

Because their love is pure and unconditional, angels are always ready and willing to assist all who request their help. In fact, they want us to ask them for help. Because of free will, angels can only help us if we ask them to—unless we are in a life-threatening situation, and it's before our time. There are many types of angels, but the two types that we work with the most are the guardian angels and archangels.

Your guardian angels are assigned to you when you are born and stay with you until you return home to the spirit world. Everyone has at least four guardian angels. Some people have more because they (or someone close to them) requested more, perhaps for health and healing or because of other important issues occurring in their lives. The role of the guardian angels is to support, encourage, and protect us on all levels. The archangels are larger in size and more powerful than the rest of the angels. They are, in fact, leaders who oversee the guardian angels and the entire angelic realm. There are hundreds upon thousands of archangels, but only 15 to 20 work closely with us on Earth. Because they are very powerful beings who have strong healing and teaching powers, more and more archangels are coming forward to work with us now. All archangels have specialties, and the archangel with the most appropriate specialty is the one who will show up to help when requested.

Many times, angels show up in forms we don't expect. For example, my mother conducted a reading long ago for a woman who handed her a silver coin. As my mother held the coin, a feeling of impending doom overwhelmed her. Feelings of abdominal pain, intense fear, and physical death followed.

"This coin holds death," my mother told the woman, who then told my mother to put the coin down and go wash her hands and then she would tell her something about the coin. My mother did this, and when she returned to the table, the woman then told her an amazing story. Years earlier, the woman's six-year-old son was playing in the front yard while the woman was in the kitchen. When the boy's ball rolled into the street, he ran to retrieve it without looking. The woman then heard a horrendous crash and ran out to find that a milk truck had hit her son. He was bleeding badly from his mid-section, and his injuries appeared life-threatening. Someone called an ambulance, and a crowd of people gathered around the scene. As the mother knelt by her son, an authoritative man in a black suit suddenly appeared standing over them. He bent down and handed the boy a silver coin.

"Squeeze this coin when it hurts," he told the boy. No one paid much attention to the man, who promptly disappeared into the crowd.

The boy grasped the coin and held it all the way to the hospital until the nurses had to pry it out of his little hand to take him into surgery. When he came out, his mother sat at his hospital bedside, praying he would just make it to the morning. He did, and eventually, the boy made a full recovery. The coin the stranger gave the boy was the coin the woman gave my mother to hold.

"Who was this man who gave my son the coin?" she asked my mother. "He disappeared, and no one has seen him since."

"The mysterious man in the black suit was your son's guardian angel," my mother explained. "He manifested in physical form when your son needed him, to intervene and save his life. All the energies of pain, fear, and death that were within your son were pushed into this coin, and his life was spared." As this story clearly illustrates, we are never alone, because our guardian angels are always nearby, offering protection, guidance, and unconditional love.

## Starting to Work With Your Guides

Once we meet and establish a relationship with our guides, it is important that we come to an agreement with them to work together as a team to expand our light energy as much as possible. Just because we have spirit guides does not mean that we don't have free will to do what we want. Our guides are here to guide us, not take us over or tell us what to do. We can contact them and ask for their guidance and help in three common ways—by being observant and watching for signs, through meditation, and during dreams. I'll discuss each briefly.

### Be Observant and Watch for Signs

Being aware of your surroundings so you can observe signs is a very important way of getting messages from your guides. These messages may not come in a profound or struck-by-lightning kind of way. They are most often subtle, gentle nudges that will point you in the proper direction.

For example, a song on the radio that evokes a certain feeling or memory, a chance meeting with an old friend you weren't expecting to see, something overheard in a conversation between people you don't know, reading a sentence in a book that stands out to you, or getting a nagging feeling that you should not do something are all signs that could signal a message from your spirit guide. Pay attention, because you will find that following these subtle messages could prevent many potential conflicts.

## Meditate

During meditation, you can meet your guides purposely. By clearing your mind and allowing yourself to go into a semi-trance state, you can consciously raise your vibrations just above the Earth plane to the Astral plane or higher in order to see and hear your guides. Again, don't expect this communication to come in some profound way—that doesn't always happen. The communication could be as subtle as a single word or phrase popping into your head that resonates deep within your being. Or you may just receive a picture. Learn to quiet your mind and listen to the silence during meditation.

## During Dreams

When you sleep, your Astral body is permitted to leave your physical body and travel through the different realms and dimensions. You can go as far as you like without getting lost—

you will still remain attached to your body by what is known as the Silver Cord, which will always bring you back to your physical body safe and sound. Astral travel is a normal occurrence during sleep—we all do it whether we are aware of it or not. People use Astral travel to visit different planes of existence in search of many different things. You may meet with your spirit guides, seek out deceased loved ones, or even meet with others from the Earth plane who are also traveling in the Astral plane.

Keep a dream journal so you can record your dreamtime experiences. Even if you don't understand what your dreams mean at the time, writing down as much as you can remember may be valuable later on when certain things become clear. Keeping paper and a pen or pencil on your nightstand so you can reach them easily will allow you to take notes about your experiences before they slip away.

When you meet your guides in dreams, on one level you will recognize them instantly because you have met and counseled with them before—even if you don't consciously remember. Many times the knowledge of these meetings is stored deep within your subconscious to be accessed later when the information will be useful to you.

## Layers of Messages

Especially important signs sometimes come one right after the other, and they also can have many rich layers of meaning. By looking at them carefully, you can receive further guidance with each level you recognize.

A good example is the story of what happened to me not long ago when I was battling my ex-husband in court over a child support issue. When his lawyer cross-examined me, he began with some routine questions, and then all of a sudden, he started to read the preface of this book (which was already available online). He asked me if what he was reading sounded familiar, and I answered, "Yes! You're reading from my book!" Then he asked me if I was a Lightworker, and I said yes. I was proud to say that my business helped so many people. As he continued to read from my book, I could feel the light energy expanding in the room, even though I assumed he was trying to make me sound like a nut. Then he stopped reading and asked me if I believed I had been incarnated onto Earth. I answered, "Yes of course! We all are." The judge just smiled, the lawyer's line of questioning fell flat, and we went on with the case.

I could have been angry that the lawyer was mocking my beliefs, but by staying aware of what was really happening, I could see that he was really a divine messenger. He was sending me a message from the universe to remember who I am and the enormous amount of support that is always there for me. The following week, I was on my way to meet my lawyer and was about to drive into the complex where his office is located. All of a sudden, a huge hawk with a big black rat in his talons flew out from the side of the highway and slammed into my truck! He dropped the rat in the road and kept on flying. Although he had struck the corner of my roof and windshield pretty hard, he didn't break the glass. It was such an arresting experience that I knew right away it was a sign. I took it as a message that the rat in my life, my ex, would be cast off. But then I looked deeper and got more guidance. A friend reminded me that hawk is a powerful, Native American totem that is in itself a sign that a message from Spirit is coming. Birds are masters of flight and can usually avoid vehicles—but in this case, the hawk had not fully factored in the weight of the rat. That understanding led to another message: in order to clear obstacles safely, I will *first* have to let go of whatever dead things I am carrying in my life.

Then I looked at where the hawk had hit my car—where the roof and windshield met. The roof, to me, symbolizes the highest level. This message clearly held strong spiritual importance. And the windshield is what you see out of, so the message also had to do with the importance of maintaining clear sight. Every time I peeled back another layer of the message, I got chills!

And it turned out to be just what I needed to be aware of at exactly the right time.

No matter how they come, these signs and communications from your guides will become increasingly more apparent when you learn to be more aware of them and to pay closer attention. Being unaware of a guide's or angel's presence, on the other hand, is like navigating an obstacle course with a blindfold on. Fortunately, the universe is talking to you all the time, trying to get your attention in a million different ways; all you need to do is stay aware and stay open to receiving this divine guidance.

# 8

# Empathy: Mirror, Mirror on the Wall

Susan was always the go to girl for all her friends. When a friend experienced a break up, Susan was the first one to call for advice. When her family had differences to settle, she was the one to the mend fences. She was always the one who ended up training new employees, even though that task wasn't in her job description. Susan was humble, and when someone praised her, she praised them back doubly. She always had a strong connection with animals, and they always gravitated to her, even to the extent of scratching on her front door if they were lost. She didn't watch much television and found the newspapers to be a real downer, so she wasn't current on politics or world events. She was a natural-born poet, and her words moved people deep inside. She found using her gift of creativity most helpful when she experienced her regular bouts of depression. Susan had trouble maintaining a healthy weight and often turned to comfort foods, because she often felt sudden waves of deep sadness that seemed to come out of nowhere. There were days when she couldn't even get out of bed. She found it hard to control the ups and downs of her moods; she wondered why she had to suffer so much pain.

Empathy is the ability to sense and understand the emotions of others; voluntarily or involuntarily, an Empath will immediately tune in to the emotions of someone and subconsciously even mirror the other person. They are not only sensitive to energies of others, but are also acutely aware of mannerisms and inflections in others' voices that reveal their emotional states. Many Lightworkers possess powerful empathy towards not only other people, but also animals, plants, or anything with an energy field. Empaths also have an ability to instantaneously scan another's energy field for thoughts, feelings, and experiences—from past, present, and future—and respond to them accordingly. The Empath will relate to emotions buried deep below the surface that even the person carrying may not be able to identify or understand. The Empath has the ability to sense the true nature of someone's emotional state and, acting compassionately, make an individual feel at ease and comforted.

Many Empaths are unaware of how this process actually works, and may suffer because of the strong connection they share with those around them and the collective energy of the planet. Lightworkers who rely strongly on their empathic component are descended from the fourth plane. These sensitive beings are highly aware of sight and sound and have an eye for beauty. They have a strong creative gift and can be born writers or artists with a high degree of creativity and imagination. Many empathic fourth-plane Lightworkers work towards world peace through their music or writings; John Lennon and Bob Marley were great examples of this type of Lightworker. Empaths seek out peace and harmony for all mankind, because they have a tendency to openly respond to what is around them moreso than what is inside of them. A world of peace and harmony is what they long for because such a world would bring them the deep sense of inner peace that they strive to give others.

Because empathic Lightworkers descend from the fourth plane or above, they are very responsive to sight and sound, and their sensory perceptions form how they are able to sense the pain and suffering of others. They are programmed to pick up even the most minute signal or tone that will indicate underlying emotions. A gesture, the inflection in a person's voice; or a slight change in a person's posture will all be subconscious indicators to the Empath of what is happening emotionally deep within the person with whom they are interacting. Without even realizing, the Empath will know exactly how to react to what they are seeing or hearing, perhaps even mirroring the subject and making the individual feel relaxed and understood. This ability is what makes Empaths so magnetic to others. People just gravitate to them, because they see a mirror image of themselves when they see the Empath.

## Do You Have Heightened Empathic Abilities?

Read the following list and check how many relate to you in your life:

* Strangers often approach you for assistance (asking for directions, asking for the correct time, and so on).
* You always seem to befriend or assist the new person (coworkers, people at social gatherings, and so on).
* Friends and family always come to you with their problems.
* Animals are highly drawn to you.
* Compliments embarrass you or make you feel uncomfortable.
* You meditate better with music or you find listening to music very soothing.
* People say you have a "friendly face."
* People say you are a good listener.
* You have a healing effect on others.
* You have a strong telepathic gift.

There are also many side effects to being empathic that can be problematic if you are unaware of what is occurring such as:

* Experiencing physical pain or discomfort when you hear or see someone hurt or harmed (especially in the Empath's root chakra or solar plexus).
* Being prone to unexpected bouts of depression.
* Dealing with weight issues due to indulging in comfort foods to sooth unexplained sadness.
* Exhibiting unhealthy behaviors or addictions in an effort to sooth depression, anxiety, or anger.
* Being diagnosed as bipolar/manic depressive.
* Having stomach or digestive issues.
* Experiencing sudden mood swings or outbursts of anger.
* Suffering frequent chronic fatigue, lack of energy, or exhaustion.
* Feeling suspicion or paranoia.

Without a conscious awareness of what is happening, the burden of taking in the emotions of others and taking on the emotional energy of the collective can be downright torturous for the unaware Empath. The overload of all the incoming stimulation, information, and energies brings on anxiety, depression, or any number of overwhelming disturbances in the life of the unaware Empath.

## Feeling the Effects

Many times, when there is a natural disaster or some other sudden tragic event that affects the planet, an Empath will feel the effects. Without any apparent reason, Empaths may become overwhelmed with feelings that do not relate to their own lives at the moment, sending them spiraling into a cataclysmic sea of emotions that are unwarranted. Their feelings can leave the Empath wondering why they have to suffer so much and feeling like the world is caving in on them. Carrying the burden of the emotions of the entire planet can soon begin to feel like being trapped in a living hell. Being an energetic sponge and absorbing all the misery of the planet can bring on feelings of hopelessness, despair, and desperation.

## Finding Some Relief

One way for Empaths to escape their torment is by working with their ability and their love of sight and sound. Fourth-plane Lightworkers come from a plane so rich with sight and sound that incarnates of the physical cannot even process the exquisiteness of it. Because Empaths are creative spirits who resonate with beauty on a deep soul level, it is best for them to release this tension by creating beauty. Any of the following activities can assist you in releasing empathic emotions you are taking on:

- Writing.
- Painting.
- Singing.
- Dancing.

* Sculpting.
* Arranging flowers.
* Working with clay.
* Any tactile activity.
* Creating beauty in any way.

Creating beauty of sight and sound is a big part of their purpose and when that function is left stagnant, the Empath's energy becomes blocked. This blocked energy creates the psychological and emotional breakdowns we have discussed here. Whatever resonates with the Empath personally on a creative level will immediately bring the Empath back to the soul's origin of beauty and expression. Their absorbed emotions need to be released somehow, and creative expression is a wonderful way for Empaths to release them. Empaths are here to heal the planet, but unless their own energy is maintained and kept healthy, it will be difficult to for them achieve your goals here on Earth. The Empath is a natural healer as well, and because Empaths are so connected to using their light energy to heal, allowing their energy to flow smoothly gives the Empath a feeling of contentment and a vitality for life.

# 9

# Belief Makes All Things Possible

One very important aspect to your lightwork is the power to believe. The absolute knowing that the mystical is all around us will allow you to open your mind to Source information and allow it to flow without the blocks of preconceived ideas. I was fortunate enough to be raised in an environment that supported this belief. Not only was it present in my home life, but the universe even seemed to have lovingly raised me in a town that would further enhance the knowing that anything is possible.

I didn't think I would ever tell my story. My mother told me that what I'm about to reveal will seem unbelievable to most, but that's the nature of this chapter, to believe in what seems unbelievable. I guess I should begin with my family name, which dates back to the late 18th century from a quaint village in Italy. The mere notion of a medium whose family name means "the light" seems just a bit too amazing and other-worldly, but who am I to question the unbelievable? My entire life dwells in that realm.

I come from a long line of great female mediums and psychics, and we are branches on a family tree that includes my dear great-grandmother whose married last name was LaLumia, pronounced *la-lu-me-a,* and in Italian translates to "the light."

My grandmother Grace, the mystic, who put onions in your socks to rid you of evil spirits and fevers, believed in the old ways of chants, candles, and curses and honored the name while considering it a calling card. Throughout my childhood, the women of my family would instill in me the importance of our namesake and all that it meant. The gift of bearing this name meant that we were born to share all things mystical and clarify what others called the supernatural. To us, the mystery of the spirit world was neither odd nor frightening, but it was absolutely natural and easy to explain.

Growing up as a young girl in Northern New Jersey, my mother always talked to me about the "white light." She repeatedly told me, "Sahvanna, always surround yourself with the white light." She would say this each time I would run outside to play in the earthly world.

She taught me that this was the ultimate form of protection, knowledge and power—and one that was unstoppable. I never questioned it.

At about the age of 10, I began to hear voices in the night, and they would always hover, but never seemed to really haunt me. My entire body would vibrate from the spirits that tried to enter it, but it would be quite some time before I learned how to handle them. "Leave me alone," I would tell the spirits. "Go away! I surround myself with the white light; I surround myself with the white light." I would say before I drifted off to sleep. The light is as much of who I am as is my blood, my bone, and my own spirit.

## How It All Began

Growing up, my mother, Marilyne, was quite a sensitive child who trusted and communicated with angels to provide her with knowledge and direction. She was always exceptionally advanced for her age, and is an avid reader until this day. Each Sunday she would look forward to the comic section in the weekly paper, but one Sunday, something else caught her eye. At seven or eight, she read an article on mental telepathy, and she became curious about the powers of the mind. She decided on the perfect way to test what she had read about. About a year earlier, her beloved dog, Girl, had disappeared after having puppies. Her father took Girl away when he grew tired of her endless litters of puppies. Marilyne never forgot her and dreamed of the day they would be reunited. The very next day, she repeatedly called the dog in her mind, squeezing her eyes shut and yelling as loud as she could in her mind.

On the third day, while playing in her front yard, she miraculously saw what appeared to be her dog running towards her from down the road, but the condition of the dog was less than desirable. Skinny, dirty, and with a broken chain around her neck, her dog stopped and looked at her as though she knew she had been called by the sound of her master's thoughts. The broken chain was evidence that she heard her from afar.

Sadly, her father frightened her dog again, only this time she never came back. Marilyne lost Girl again, but she was left with a new understanding of a universal connection, which she would later pass down to her children.

My mother's penchant for the metaphysical world never seemed peculiar at all. My grandmother Grace was a one-woman demon chaser who made sure that nothing evil came close to herself or her family. She believed in the ancient methods of putting curses on people who wronged you, and the healing rituals, which removed the evil spirits that would make you sick in the first place.

If you suffered from headaches, Grace would place a bowl of oil and water on your head. She believed that the spirits were attacking your head because someone gave you an insincere compliment. "The spirits are jealous, and they are making your head throb," she would whisper.

She then proceeded to place a bowl of oil and water on the head of the sufferer and make the sign of the cross again and again as she spoke in tongues. If she saw two eyes in the water (or two circles of oil), it meant that you also had the evil eye on you. Naturally, the only solution then was to wear a red ribbon and a horn around your neck to make the eye go away. More serious prayers about ridding evil spirits could only be done at midnight on Christmas Eve when Grace prayed for the wellness of her entire family for the next year. Grandmother Grace was sure that she could ward off nuisance evils such as the common cold. If your chest was filled with mucus, she defied medical science and simply put a drinking glass over the congestion and then waved a candle under the glass. White smoke would fill the glass and she would then place that on your chest. It would suck up the skin a bit from the lack of oxygen, but Grace believed that it was also sucking the cold out of your chest. If you had a fever, she cut up potatoes and onions in thick slices, put them in your socks and then placed them on your feet.

"These will draw the evil fever spirits out of your body. When the onions are cooked, the spirits will be gone," she promised. Years later when I was born and had a kidney infection with a high fever, my mother gave me antibiotics. My grandmother put onions in my socks and I smelled for a week. Nothing seemed abnormal about all this to us. My Grandmother's home was always filled with paranormal activity.

For Christmas in 1967, my mother had given her brother Joey a Ouija board as a gift. He was just a teen and was fascinated by the paranormal. He loved to hear his big sister talk about ghosts and haunted houses. One day in early January, they decided to try this new "toy." Sitting at the kitchen table, Joey wondered just what this thing was all about and if it would be powerful. They placed their hands on it and waited. To their shock, it began to move. "Who are you?" they asked, "Who's this?"

The planchette started to move swiftly and they could barely keep up with the spelling. "My name is Achak."

"Where are you?" they asked and were starting to get giddy at the way the planchette was flying around the board.

"I am here."

"Where?"

"Here, in the kitchen with you," the spirit explained, adding that he was of American Indian decent and he died at the age of 12 when he went to the river to gather water for his family.

He explained how he had slid off a narrow ridge and fell to his death. They wanted proof that the spirit of this Indian boy was really there in the kitchen with them.

"Prove you are here; show us," they begged.

Soon the spirit went on to direct them to certain things around the house. "Go into the cupboard and you will find three pennies, and a buffalo head nickel," The spirit instructed.

Joey ran to the cupboard as directed. Sure enough, there were the three pennies and a buffalo head nickel. Achak had another assignment for Joey and told him to go into the second bedroom down the hallway where he should look under the bed and he would find three tennis balls and a crumbled up piece of paper with these words on it: "Michele (my twelve year old cousin) Theme paper." Joey ran down the hallway with my mother following closely on his heels. Swooping under his bed, he retrieved a piece of paper, uncrumpled it and saw the clear, black wording of *Michele, theme paper*. Then he retrieved four tennis balls.

"But you said three tennis balls!" Joey told the spirit.

"I didn't see that one; it was too far back under the bed!" Achak spelled out on the talking board. The games continued for hours. Could this be? Was there really the spirit of a young Indian boy in the house with them?

Some six months before, young Joey went with his father on a construction job and had unearthed a small skull while they dug on the site. It appeared to be a human child the size of about a 10 year old. Perhaps it was an Indian burial ground, because the area had a history of Indians. Could this be the skull of Achak? Did the skull in the basement have a chance to introduce itself through the talking board? For Joey and my mother, this was becoming too real, and it was kind of amusing. Because the spirit was happy and playful, they felt no fear. He joked with them and played tricks for hours. Both my mother and Joey were having so much fun with the spirit they didn't want to stop playing with the board—until the spirit's playfulness began to change. Suddenly Achak's tone changed and a certain feeling of evil filled the room. The spirit began to cry out for help. Repeatedly, he began spelling out, "I pain, I pain," over and over on the board. "What happened?

What's wrong?" they asked.

"Danger; evil here, and I cannot protect you," the spirit warned. The laughter and games came to an abrupt end as this light, playful spirit was being attacked by some dark entity. Suddenly, the planchette flew from their hands and shot across the table and hit the kitchen wall. My mother said Joey took the board outside and broke it into pieces and wanted nothing more to do with Ouija boards.

Something remained in the house that was evil and dark. Joey passed away in a tragic drowning accident only a few months later at the age of fifteen. That was just the first of many bizarre and tragic events that occurred during the 50 years my family owned that house. Eventually, after my grandparents' passing, the house was passed down to me. My family did not stay there long. It was only about a year before I found a note in our mailbox that read "If you're interested in selling your house, call me." The unprovoked offer caught my interest, and I called the number on the note. The woman Lola explained to me that she had contracted to buy another two-family home down the street, but the deal fell through.

Our home was very similar and she thought we might be interested in a good offer. I took her up on it and sold her the house. It was only about a year and half later I was told that she hanged herself off the dark staircase in the hallway that lead to the downstairs apartment. It was chilling news and I thanked my guides for getting us out of there as quickly as possible. The legacy of this house was marked with some tragic events and an extreme amount of paranormal activity.

## The Ouija in the Cupboard

In my own home with my brother, sister, and I, my mother would take out the Ouija board and conduct mediumship readings for a growing list of friends and neighbors who heard that my mother could reach out to the great beyond. The Ouija board was a fixture in my home and blended in unobtrusively next to the toaster. When my mother worked the Ouija board, I noticed I could always hear the spirit's messages in my head before they got a chance to spell out the words with the planchette, an early sign of my mediumship potentials. My mother was also amazing at automatic writing and the pen in her hand seemed to take on a life as it stringed words together in sentences with no breaks. Like a little psychic sponge, I absorbed all of this and became educated to the ways of the mystical as if it was nothing unusual. When I was three, I linked to the spirit world for the first time.

Being an extremely sensitive child, I knew my mother's pain was severe after the loss of Joey. I was too young to remember him, and never really saw a photo of him because it was too difficult for my mother to have reminders around our house. Yet, one day I came out of my bedroom after writing with pen all over my arm, which was an activity I was usually forbidden to do. My Mom looked at me, and I said, "Mommy, Uncle Joey told me to do this. He is here. He came to see me in my room." She gasped when the markings on my arm resembled a drawing he had done of a cross with complicated patterns and inlaid designs.

"Uncle Joey came to see me," I explained.

A year later, my mother was conducting psychic readings for a cousin, and I was under the table playing with my magic 8-ball. I was four years old and shaking the magic 8-ball, while I listened as my mother prophesied.

"You're going to California," I stated in a clear voice from my spot on the cold linoleum.

"What is she talking about?" my cousin asked my mother.

A week later, she called and reported in amazement that her boss had called her into his office. He wanted her to transfer to a bigger role in another office...in another state. She packed her bags and left for California. All this seemed completely natural to me because I was raised with the belief that this *was* normal.

## A Place to Belong

When I was seven years old, we moved to a shingled colonial home in northern New Jersey that must have dated back to the Revolutionary War. It was nestled in a humble valley in the Ramapo Mountains, which were a part of the Appalachian Trail of upstate New York. There is something very magical and mystical about the Ramapo Mountains.

No one was sure of the exact age of the home my parents purchased in the early 1970s, because the deed stated "unknown." We were all quite excited to be moving to the country. There were mountains, lakes, and fields as far as the eye could see and my grandparents now lived right across the street from us. Once we moved, there was an unofficial promise of a happy life because our previous homes were small, rented apartments. Now our future seemed bright with both a home and a yard to play in that we could call our own. My parents could not have chosen a better community. The crime rate was nonexistent, except for the two kids who (in a mischievous act gone terribly wrong), climbed to the roof of a pizzeria and fired off a shotgun towards the town hall across the street. With freakish accuracy the shot struck and killed the judge who was residing court at the time! This *Ripley's Believe it Or Not!* type of incident gave our town a spot on the front page of the *Daily News*, but it wasn't the only out-of-this-world tale that gave the small town a place in history. The town I grew up in was always a blue-collar town with middle-class folks just like us, who valued family and tradition, but it also had a very strong mystical undertone, with rich Native American history and folklore legends. Growing up, the events that occurred in our town not only bolstered my belief that the mystical always surrounded us, but beckoned to me to seek it out.

## Close Encounters of the Second Kind

When I was a young girl, I would hear stories from my grandfather about events that occurred surrounding a nearby reservoir, the picturesque lake just minutes from my home. A newspaper article read:

* * * *

> January 11, 1966 started like any other mid-winter day in the small suburban town. The air was clear and cold, kids were enjoying the holiday vacation from school, and residents of the borough went about their usual daily routines. Little did they know that before the day was over something would happen, something fantastic and unexplainable that would change the lives of many of the townsfolk forever.

One early evening, on a winter night, police began to receive reports of a glowing, fiery round object hovering above the water of the reservoir. It bobbed and hovered there as not only the police watched, but residents gathered to stare in awe. My Uncle Joe and Grandfather, who lived minutes away, raced there to have seen it in the sky as well. It was reported that police began to receive calls from towns within a 20-mile radius reporting this unidentified flying object.

Police and townsfolk alike were then stunned as they watched the object land on the frozen water and burn a hole right through the ice. There were other sightings within the next few days and then the activity stopped. No one could ever explain what the mysterious spinning, glowing light was, and to this day, curiosity seekers visit the site, waiting for perhaps another celestial visitor to appear. It was well-known by everyone in the town that the government would regularly send researchers to the area to set up equipment and study the site. The incident was recognized by many UFO researchers as an authentic sighting and even after all these years is known as the "Roswell of the Ramapos."

# Mysterious Mountains

My grandfather loved the Ramapo Mountains and, even at an advanced age, continued to hike and visit the mountains often. He loved them so much, in fact, at his request, when he passed in 2003, his ashes were scattered there on the mountain ridge. The mountains just vibrate with the energy of the Native Americans who once resided there. One visit my grandfather took through the hiking trails proved that the forces watching over the mountain were not to be taken lightly.

## Guardians at the Gate

Right on Ramapo ridge, just before the entrance of the Wanaque Reservoir Dam area, are the ruins of the house known as the "Van Slyke Castle." The house, the lake, and surrounding area have interesting histories themselves, but the original Van Slyke Castle, known as Foxcroft, was built in the late 1800s and, for reasons unknown, left abandoned in the 1950s.

Eventually vandals broke in and torched the castle in 1959. Since its destruction, the ruins have remained there for curious visitors to explore and imagine what the elegant structure was like in its glory days. The stone walls, fireplaces, and foundations that still stand are now overgrown and covered in ivy.

One spring afternoon, my grandfather took my brother Rick and my Uncle Joey up there to hike the beautiful trails through the Ramapo Forest. As they approached the area of the castle, my grandfather heard something making its way through the brush. He told the boys to stop, and they stood on the trail in silence, waiting to see what appeared. A few moments passed by and they saw nothing. My grandfather gave the boys the go-ahead to walk forward on the trail to the castle.

As they proceeded, my grandfather spotted a pack of wild dogs running out of the woods onto the trail from the castle. He described them as wolves, gray and white, with ears that stood erect. He described their growling like the sounds of demons out of hell as they came toward them. They lunged at the boys and attacked them viciously, taking hold of both the boy's limbs and shaking their heads in an act of prey drive that was meant to kill. My grandfather grabbed one dog by the scruff of the neck and took out his pocket knife. He said the head of the dog spun around in his grip and looked at him with pure evil in its eyes. Before my grandfather could stab it, the vicious dogs retreated and took off down the trail. The boys had been knocked to the ground and were stunned, "Are you ok?" my grandfather asked, out of breath.

"Yeah, Gramps," My brother looked at his sleeves, "they had no teeth!" my brother said.

"No teeth!" Joey reported the same thing! Not a mark on the boys.

The guardians of the VanSlyke Castle had issued a stern warning: stay away or else. My grandfather said he and the boys turned and decided not to visit the castle or hike the trail that day.

## A Portal to Another Dimension

The Vortex is located just passed the reservoir dam on a long dirt road that has been cleared in a wooded area. We have hiked up there many times and the eerie vibrations can be felt by anyone who dares to enter the area. My mother told me that the location was once where cannonballs were brought to soldiers who camped in the spot during the Revolutionary War.

As a medium, each time I have gone up there I have heard the echoes of soldier's voices or sounds of metal clanking. There are still some spirits lingering in the area from the war. In fact, one day while visiting the Vortex, I came face-to-face with the spirit of a Revolutionary War soldier in full gear. He appeared to be digging a grave. I tried to dialogue with him, but he would not communicate with me. He just continued digging. But the history of the area goes deeper than the war. It is said the site of the Vortex is also on an Indian burial ground which was disrupted when DuPont placed an explosives plant there after World War I. From the very start, the plant was to be plagued by disaster. In 1917, 400,000 pounds of smokeless powder exploded at the plant. The explosion (that rocked the area for miles) killed several people.

The unofficial theory is that between the energies of the spirits trapped there (from the War and the Indian burial ground) and the deposits of chemicals from the DuPont company, the ground was activated and an electromagnetic field was created, creating a vortex or portal to other dimensions. Observers have reported seeing dragons, tree sprites, angels, and other entities there. Many people have documented and studied the area. Orbs, mysterious figures, and otherworldly beings from ancient civilizations are said to emerge from the ground and have been spotted at the Vortex. One researcher even claims to have connected and communicated with a group of Astral plane beings that call themselves Endorians who act as sentinels and guard the grounds.

## The Mysterious Ramapo Mountain People

The Ramapo Mountains seemed to be home to the unusual and growing up in the shadows of this mystical mountain not only fueled my curiosity for the metaphysical but beckoned for me to seek it out. The Mountain is also home to a mysterious community of people called the Ramapo Mountain People or Jackson Whites (not a name they prefer). These people have lived an isolated existence tucked away in the Ramapo Mountains for hundreds of years. It is said that these people are descendants of runaway slaves, Dutch settlers, and rogue Hessian soldiers who had deserted the British during the American Revolution. After the end of the war, they fled the frontier areas of the mountains and have remained in the woods for hundreds of years. Frozen in time, these outcasts spent an isolated existence in shacks with no electricity or heat within the old mining areas of Northern New Jersey. In the early 1980's, the government stepped in to provide funding to modernize their unsafe living conditions. At this time, some of the children began to attend public school, and I became friendly with several of them. My curiosity of their secret society urged me to seek out these kids and get more information. I did befriend a girl named April and she shared with me the mysteries of their lives tucked away deep in the old mine area. Eventually, she trusted me enough to invite me to her home; during one visit I had a strange experience.

It was a typical day as we sat in April's room and talked about the normal things, school, boys, and just teenage girl talk when she excused herself from the room to get a drink. I sat on her bed, gazing out her window, when a small boy approached the window from outside. I waved, and because it was a warm spring afternoon, the window was already open. "Where's April?" he asked and seemed in a rush. "She's here, she'll be right back," I said.

"Tell her Smoochie needs her to come outside, we're playing ball." Then as quickly as he appeared, he seemed to be gone.

When April returned to the room, just moments later, I relayed the message. "A little boy came to the window, Smoochie, he wants you to come outside and play ball," I said.

April looked puzzled.

"Smoochie?" I asked. Did I get the message wrong?

"Smoochie is dead," she said, just like that.

"What do you mean dead? He was just at the window... about five years old?" I said.

Then April began to tell me about her cousin, who she nicknamed Smoochie, who died in a fire about five years earlier. She said they had no heating system in the shack they lived in and a kerosene heater they were using ignited and set the house on fire, killing six children, including five-year-old Smoochie. She recalled the scene of the children hanging out the second-story window screaming for help. There was no way for the fire department to get up there and certainly no fire hydrants. She recalled the horror of seeing the children disappear from the window when the second-story floor collapsed; there was nothing anyone could do to save them. This incident finally prompted the government to intervene and update the living conditions of the Ramapo Mountain People, who had been living in shacks for years with no modern amenities. April then began to tell me how she was haunted by Smoochie and her other cousins who perished in the fire, that she heard their playful laughter outside her window all the time.

Looking back, I can understand why Smoochie reached out to me. Not fully understanding my mediumship gifts at the time, the incident was kind of creepy, but April must have been a budding medium as well, and my communication with Smoochie validated her belief that the children were still around. April and I found this as evidence that the children would never leave until someone released them. The Ramapo Mountain People had deep spiritual beliefs rooted in their Native American ancestry. About a week later, April and I conducted an Afterlife Ceremony, a Native American ritual that would ensure the children move on and not roam the area any longer. As we sat in circle in the dirt, during the ceremony, I witnessed the ethereal bodies of six children rise above a fire pit and then seem to disappear into the smoke. The children were released and April never heard the playful laughter outside her window again.

## The Power to Believe

For me, these stories are part of my life, my history. I was raised to believe and never doubt that anything is possible. That there are beings or creatures that exist in other dimensions and we can communicate with them. That loved ones never cease to exist and that we all share the same life force, living or dead. A Lightworker with no belief in the mystical world is lost. Our unseen counterparts are with us at all times, both the seen and the unseen worlds come together in a place that connects us all through Source. As you read, you think, you process, and you wonder about the possibilities. Many people never had the chance to explore what seemed unreal because their upbringing or society wouldn't allow it. Today, as we experience this tremendous shift in consciousness, we all finally get a chance to believe. We can believe in magic, in fairy tales, or in ghosts that go bump in the night, it doesn't matter. There is healing power in believing, belief in the infinite power of Source, the infinite power of ourselves and the universe that has been created for us. Believing makes all things possible and when all things are possible, we can achieve anything.

# Part III:

# Living Unencumbered

# 10

# Coming Out of the Lightworker Closet

Much of the information that I am sharing with you may seem vaguely familiar, or much of it may rcsonate deeply within your soul. If reading the information presented in this book creates a stirring in your being, you may be experiencing an awakening of your dormant Lightworker soul, and now is the time to begin the journey of your life's work. As you begin to remember the promise that you made before coming to Earth, you will come to understand that your life has divine purpose. Many Lightworkers struggle in their lifetimes; many of you may have had traumatic or unhappy lives before you finally reached the point of realization. You will have been tempted, tested, and pushed into the dark night of the soul; but Lightworkers always have the ability to rise above the darkness and emerge spiritually progressed, ready to share their light energy. My dark period lasted almost 10 years. After my father transitioned, my faith was tested and I became unsure of my purpose. The road back was long, but it brought me to the time and place at which I needed to be in order to begin my work here on Earth.

## Beautiful but Broken Spirits

If you take notice of some of the famous Lightworkers mentioned in Chapter 3, you will see many led painful and difficult lives. Some of these famous Lightworkers were so filled with light energy they simply could not adjust to the heaviness of the Earth plane. They felt they never belonged, and they wanted to go home. Many left us and never knew the impact of their gifts on the world. Here are some examples:

> **Abraham Lincoln** (February 12, 1809–April 15, 1865): From the 3rd plane. Served as the 16th President of the United States from March 1861 until his assassination in April 1865. Led the country through its greatest internal crisis, the American Civil War; preserved the Union; and ended slavery, freeing an entire race. Abraham suffered severe depression and wrote "I am now the most miserable man living, if what I feel were equally distributed to the whole human family, there would not be one cheerful face on the Earth. Whether I shall ever be better I cannot tell; I awfully forebode I shall not. To remain as I am is impossible; I must die or be better, it appears to me."

> **Frida Kahlo** (July 6, 1907–July 13, 1954): From the 4th plane. A Mexican artist who was born with spina bifida, contracted polio at age six, suffered traumatic

injuries, miscarriages, and more than most could ever bear throughout her life. Kahlo's work is remembered for its "pain and passion," and it seemed to be the way of her entire life. She wrote days before her death "I hope the exit is joyful—and I hope never to return—Frida." Frida died at age 47 of a pulmonary embolism, although some suspected that she died from an overdose which may not have been accidental.

**Vincent Van Gogh** (March 30, 1853–July 29, 1890): From the 4th plane. A Dutch post-Impressionist painter. He suffered from anxiety and increasingly frequent bouts of mental illness throughout his life and died, unknown, at the age of 37 from a self-inflicted gunshot wound. He wrote his brother Theo saying that he "died for the greatest good of all." He never knew the impact his work would have on the world.

**Virginia Woolf** (January 25, 1882–March 28, 1941): From the 4th plane. English author, essayist, publisher, writer of short stories, and feminist. Virginia suffered depression and was a victim of sexual abuse. On March 28, 1941, Woolf put on her overcoat, filled its pockets with stones, and walked into the River Ouse near her home and drowned. She wrote to her husband: "I feel certain that I am going mad again. I feel we can't go through another of those terrible times. And I shan't recover this time. I begin to hear voices, and I can't concentrate. So I am doing what seems the best thing to do. You have given me the greatest possible happiness. You have been in every way all that anyone could be. I can't fight any longer."

**Diana, Princess of Wales** (Diana Frances Spencer; July 1, 1961–August 31, 1997): From the 3rd plane. A member of the British royal family and loved by the world in the late 20th century as the first wife of Charles, Prince of Wales, whom she married on July 29, 1981. Diana led a sad and lonesome life and was known as "The People's Princess" She suffered from severe depression, anorexia, bulimia, her husband's countless infidelities, and suicide attempts, yet she worked tirelessly for many who were in need, comforting those dying of AIDS and serving as an International Red Cross VIP volunteer to assist victims of landmines in Angola. Diana was quoted as saying she knew she would be separate from the herd. Her intuition told her that her life was "going to be a winding road. I always felt very detached from everyone else, that I was in the wrong shell." On August 31, 1997, Diana was killed in a car accident in the Pont de l'Alma road tunnel in Paris.

**Rembrandt Bugatti** (October 16, 1884–January 8, 1916): From the 4th plane. An Italian sculptor, known primarily for his bronze sculptures of wildlife subjects. Rembrandt volunteered as a paramedic aide at the Red Cross Military Hospital in Antwerp. His experiences among the sick and dying caused the sensitive artist to lapse into depression during World War I. Finally, when the Antwerp Zoo was forced to kill most of its wild livestock, this deeply affected him because he had used many of these animals as objects for his sculptures, and in 1916, at the age of 31, he killed himself.

* * * *

It's apparent how all these beautiful Lightworkers suffered so much pain just to share their gifts with the world. How tragic that while they were here, they never knew how their beautiful light energy contributed to the healing of the planet. Most of them thought the world would be a better place without them in it. These are just a few examples, but the list could go on and on. It is not uncommon for a Lightworker to suffer from mental, emotional, or even physical issues. Due to their high degree of sensitivity, they are just prone to these types of challenges. Still, they do not need to be a tragic figure to shine their light on the world. Lightworkers can learn to balance and manage their heightened components to control the overloads. When Lightworkers understand their true purpose and the nature of their own complexities, it becomes easier to cope with life here on Earth.

## Is It Your Time?

The day may come that you will awaken to your divine purpose, want to go "public" with your lightwork and begin a spiritual practice to help others. Being of service helps to keep the light energy of the Earth expanding, and there are many different ways to accomplish this. Lightworkers will find that they are called to a certain area of work. Discovering their plane of origin (see Chapter 3) will help with this.

This is a wonderful milestone to which you have come in your development. As a Lightworker, you have been contracted to use certain gifts to help to heal the Earth plane. There is no need to worry about being ready. I firmly believe that the universe will bring you to this point of working with others, but only when you are ready. If you go there, and it is not your time, I promise, you will surely find yourself blocked. Obstacles will come your way to prevent you from working with the public, and you will eventually stop trying until the time is right.

On the other hand, when the time is right, the universe will clear the path like a bulldozer to help you to do your work, and together you will construct an environment that will enable you to be highly effective in your service to mankind. The Spirit will create signs and synchronicities in your life that will leave no doubt in your mind as to what directions to take. In retrospect, you will be amazed at the steps through which the universe has taken you to get to the place at which you need to be. If you follow this divine compass blindly and have absolute trust, you will never take the wrong path.

As your dedication to your lightwork builds, you will also find yourself surrounded by others who want to be of service and also only have the highest intentions. As you increase your light quotient here on Earth, your high vibrational level will be enough to clear out those whose intentions are not aligned with the greatest good of all. When you do find yourself at the point at which you want to work with others as a Lightworker, it is time to keep your channel clear at all times, and consider yourself a beacon of light for the world. After you have successfully harnessed your Lightworker heightened components, you can begin to function openly in a service capacity. You may have a fascination or intense interest in one area of lightwork, and this is a strong signal that this is the work that you have been sent here to do. This is the spirit's message to you; this calling is your life's purpose.

## Set Your Intentions

When you begin your lightwork, it is important to set your intentions and have a clear idea of what you want to achieve. A true Lightworker is not a "fortune teller" who simply tells people what will happen next. Lightworkers will guide those who come to them to their highest spiritual potential. They cannot help but to do this because they are the bearers of light for the world, and are internally programmed to spread light. A Lightworker will not only assist in identifying outcomes, but will enlighten the paths of others' soul journeys. The fortune teller psychic and the Lightworker psychic perform two distinctly different practices. I would not brush the fortune teller off as insignificant; just something different. As long as the fortune telling is done with high intentions, it can be a useful tool. As a Lightworker, you should be providing healing energy and helping others to learn how to use the tools of the universe in order to gather knowledge and understanding of their own soul journeys, showing them that sometimes the powerful message lies not within the answers, but in identifying the questions that we need to be asking ourselves.

### Energy Healing

A person's energy can be damaged by traumatic or painful experiences. Wounds of the past, if not properly treated, will fester, and contaminate and block energy.

These wounds could be current or past lifetime soul injuries. Just as our physical bodies can be harmed, our spiritual bodies can also suffer traumatic injury. When our energy is harmed in some way, it is unable to flow properly. It becomes stagnant, thus perhaps actually causing the physical body to become ill. As an energy healer, you would go deep into the energy field of your client and create a healthy flow of energy. There are many ways in which this can be done, and it depends on the practitioner's technique of preference. There are many different modalities of energy healing, all of which work on the same premise: to clear or unblock stagnant energy within the physical and Astral body. This is done in any number of ways. Some modalities "treat" the affected body part with direct touch, while others do not touch the physical body at all, but instead work on clearing out the layers of the aura. Of course, there are many techniques from different cultures around the world that have been practiced for centuries.

## Animal Communicator

As a Lightworker, you will always feel a strong connection on some level with all life forms, and this includes our friends from the animal kingdom. Many Lightworkers feel a special affinity towards animals. As our companions, guides, and soulmates, our pets contribute so much to our spiritual journey. Animals can be our greatest teachers here on the Earth plane, and their role should be respected as such. As an animal communicator, you will telepathically tap into a universal language that opens up a dialogue with animals. Your heightened awareness will recognize body language and underlying signals that reveal the thoughts of our pets. Lightworkers who have strong empathic abilities are wonderful animal communicators.

You will also find that as a Lightworker, animals will automatically be drawn to you because they have an innate sense of your awareness of your own connection to the universe and to all living creatures. This ability is valuable for pet owners and animal lovers who wish to better understand their pets' needs, health issues or behavior challenges. Your connection with the animal will automatically enable you to understand what the animal is feeling, and translate the animal's verbiage so that it can be understood by the human consciousness. Animal communicators have the necessary task of bringing awareness to those here on Earth that there is a connection between all forms of life.

## Past-life Regression Therapist/Reader

This is a technique that recovers memories of past lives or incarnations. Techniques used during past-life regression are answering a series of questions, or envisioning situations that reveal events of past lives. Traumatic past-life events will carry over into current lifetimes and inhibit the spiritual progress of an individual. As a past-life therapist, you will assist others in identifying these past-life issues during your sessions. As a past-life reader, you will use your heightened components to discover past-life events for your clients, and relay the information to them. The knowledge of past-life issues or situations brings much self-realization and growth to the person receiving the information. This information will be utilized to overcome emotional blocks and healing in the present lifetime.

## Medical Intuitive

A medical intuitive is a psychic or intuitive who can energetically read the organs, glands, blood, and so on of our bodies. This work is done by intuitively scanning the body (usually starting from the top of the head and working your way down the body) for areas that may need treatment. Often, medical intuitives will be able to identify energy blockages, possibly identify the connection of an event or situation causing the illness, and relay this information to their client. They often report seeing black or dark colorations in the area or areas that are in need of treatment. This information can then be provided to the client's medical doctor and/ or health care professional for further evaluation and discussion of possible treatments. Many medical intuitive work with (or are themselves) medical doctors.

## Intuitive Advisor for Corporations or Individuals

An intuitive advisor is someone who uses his/her intuitive gifts to help those in the professional or corporate world. Presidents or CEOs of large companies and any other types of professionals can utilize intuitive advisors to make important decisions. The intuitive advisor will use his/her heightened intuition to help identify the most favorable path for a company to take in order to succeed or expand. An intuitive advisor can be utilized to assist in personal issues as well, offering clients insight into difficult questions.

# Choose Your Calling

It will be your choice as to how you share your light energy with the world. If you choose not to go into these types of practices, remember that lightwork involves many other things. Beautifying the Earth with your creative abilities, sharing your gift through writing, creating music, or advocating for those who are in need are all ways to work with the public and expand the light energy of the planet. All Lightworkers are unique with unique healing gifts to offer the Earth. Find the path that feels right for you, allow the light energy to flow through you without resistance, and you will be fulfilling your divine mission.

# 11

# Proper Care and Feeding of the Lightworker Soul

To effectively complete your mission and stay connected to your divine self (after gaining control of your heightened components), you must remember to always take care of yourself. If your own energy is not flowing freely, you will not be able to help others to your greatest potential. You will begin to lose focus and quickly become drained, making your work less effective. You are the channel for light, and if the channel is not clear, then your light energy will be blocked. Mind, body and spirit must all remain clean, clear, and focused. Body, mind, and spirit must be maintained, as well as living spaces, relationships, and personal energy fields on a regular basis.

## Energy Blockers in Your Home

Hoarding and cluttering creates energy blocks in your environment. It is essential to periodically go through your things and remove what no longer serves you or suits you in the current phase of your life. I find the best time to do the major clearing of your home is at the time of the summer and winter solstice (June and December) because these are both times of renewed energy. Each item in your home holds energy, and outdated articles of clothing, papers, and knick knacks create energetic clutter. Keeping items from the past will clog up your home's energy flow, and affect your personal energy flow. It is important to periodically go through your things and remove objects that hold outdated energy. It may be uncomfortable or even painful to part with certain items because they often represent behavior patterns or ideals that are no longer useful to you, but which you are refusing to let go. Releasing these items will assist you in releasing behavior patterns associated with them that inhibit your growth and literally drag you down like baggage as you try to move forward. Reciting the phrase "I now release that which no longer serves my highest purpose" as you pack up the items will help as you go through the releasing process. Bless the items and donate what is useful to charity or to friends who can utilize them to renew their own energy. For a Lightworker, it is essential to keep a clean, free-of-clutter flow of energy moving through your environment.

## Avoid Energy Drains

This involves people in your life who will drain you of your light energy. There are certain people referred to as "psychic vampires," because they are very needy by nature. These individuals need to draw vital energy from outside sources. Because the Lightworker omits an excessive amount of light energy, they will naturally be drawn to you. These individuals will be easy to identify because you will literally feel physically, mentally, and emotionally drained after you encounter them. If you feel that a certain loved one, friend, client or any other person in your environment drains you in this way, you must immediately disconnect yourself and use the shielding exercise that we discussed in Chapter 5, or one similar to it. You may also conduct a spiritual cleansing by taking a sea salt bath, or simply picturing yourself in a crystal clear waterfall. As the water falls over you, your spirit will be cleansed of the negative after-effects of the encounter with the psychic vampire.

Your natural Lightworker reaction may be to feel sympathy for this person, but keep in mind that you must work for the greater good of all, and being depleted of your energy does not serve the community of mankind as a whole. Other energy drains can include work environments, living arrangements, and any number of unhealthy activities that leave you depleted.

## Stay Physically Active

To keep your energy flowing, you need to avoid sedentary living. Keeping your physical body stagnated or in poor condition will affect you both emotionally and spiritually. Maintaining a regular exercise routine will help you to release excess energies or stresses that you may accumulate from your heightened components. Different activities can help you in different ways. Walking or jogging outdoors will allow you to stay grounded and connected to the Earth plane. As your feet connect with the ground, it literally will keep you connected to the Earth plane. Swimming and water activities will cleanse your aura and dilute dark energies that you may be harboring at the end of the day.

Taking a dance class will help you to express and release pent-up creative energies. Remembering that you are comprised of energy, and energy cannot be stagnant. It is essential to your overall well-being. Allowing your physical body ways to keep a proper flow and release of energy will allow your Lightworker soul to stay content in the skin that it's in while here on Earth.

## Live in Moderation

Lack of moderation creates an unbalanced life. The Lightworker who is not balanced will quickly lose focus and become unhappy. If you are working on your lightwork and do not take equal time to enjoy yourself and release tension, you're headed for a meltdown. As healers and caregivers, we sometimes forget to stop and take time to have fun. Allow your inner child to take the reins and go out and have fun! Roll in a pile of leaves, go to a pet store and play with the puppies, or sit quietly outside and count the stars. You need the down time just as much as you need to shine your light. This also goes for excesses in lifestyle and behavior patterns.

Live within your means so that you are not financially stressed. Once you begin to focus on financial worries, your focus is now shifted, and your Lightworker gift of awareness becomes dimmed. I like to envision that I am on a small boat, and if I do not throw all that is not necessary overboard, it will quickly sink! This allows me to realize the difference between what I really need and what is just excess baggage that I actually have to pay for to maintain. It keeps me free of financial stress and keeps my life uncomplicated. Overeating and drinking will almost always throw your Lightworker equilibrium off kilter, so easy does it. Living in moderation is the key to staying focused and balanced and allows you to achieve your goals much more easily.

## Practice Self-Love and Self-Acceptance

We have discussed that Lightworkers have a divine mission here on Earth. This sounds pretty heavy and may be thought of as something to live up to. Whether or not you consider yourself a Lightworker, there is no need to place unnecessary or unrealistic expectations on yourself. This only creates feelings of failure and low self-esteem when you inevitably fall short. Loving and accepting ourselves for who we are today, here and now, will help us to be better in the future. Allowing yourself the privilege of being you, and loving yourself unconditionally without boundaries, will eventually propel you to higher spiritual ground. If we practice the Lightworker component of belief, we will come to understand that Source guides us only to where we are supposed to be. No misstep is ever wasted; they are all just lessons in disguise! Be willing to take risks and trust that the universe responds only with the greatest good for all at all times. Don't fear retribution from others or the universe if you should make a mistake or experience failure. Source loves and accepts you unconditionally and so should you!

## Embracing Your Dark Days

Living in the light does not mean that you will never have dark days. As we have discussed in this book, the Lightworker is prone to more dark days than anyone else. Those who shine the brightest light walk through the darkest caverns. Allowing yourself to embrace your dark times will help you to process them with acceptance and love. I see all these self-help books that give us the secrets of how to be happy and fulfill our dreams as basically useless, because without our darkest days, we would never know true happiness. The most growth occurs when we emerge from darkness, not from walking around deliriously happy all the time! So if you're feeling sad or going through a difficult time, embrace the experience. Allow yourself to feel every moment of it, live in it without avoidance, and bless the process.

You will soon emerge into the light, I promise!

## Find Support

It is important to seek out others whose intentions are aligned with your own so that they can support you. Many Lightworkers find themselves feeling isolated or as though they just don't fit in anywhere, and some Lightworkers avoid the company of others for fear of being misunderstood or ridiculed. If you discover other like- (or light-) minded people, you will not have to hide or worry about being laughed at because of your beliefs. I have experienced it, and many times I felt that I could not be my true self because others would not understand. Suppressing my authentic self caused me great stress and sadness. It will be helpful for you to seek out groups in your area who have similar intentions as yourself. If you cannot find a group close by that you feel comfortable with, the universe understands all this and has given us a very creative way to connect with others all over the world—the Internet! We can now reach across the globe to others who share our beliefs. We now have the ability to seek out groups, Websites, or forum boards all over the world to connect and share. You'll find that there are millions like you and there is no need to suffer alone anymore.

## Allow Yourself to Be Compensated

Many Lightworkers or those on the spiritual path feel guilty for charging for their services. Being a Lightworker does not mean that you are supposed to give all of yourself and never be compensated for it. For example, if you work at building a spiritual practice, it's okay to be paid for your services. The universe seeks balance at all times, and where is the balance if you are not in some way compensated for your work? You *can* live in abundance while living your passion. It will be difficult to help others if you live in poverty and don't have enough to survive. You need to eat, live, and function here in the world. If there is somehow an equitable exchange for your services, then it is perfectly fine to charge. If the exchange is not money, perhaps you could barter services or goods. It doesn't matter, as long as it is fair and equitable. Practitioners who overcharge and take advantage of their clients will soon be out of business. The universe is a fair and accurate bookkeeper!

## Live Your Passion

When you find your calling, do not be afraid to seek it out! There may be times when you feel that the odds are stacked against you, but don't give up. The universe may seem to throw obstacles in your path, but it is only beckoning you to search for the ways around it! I always feel that when I hit a road block, it is only because there is something better down another path; and I search for that path. If you have a passion, that is your soul resonating with your purpose; don't put it aside because of fear. Embrace your gifts and share them!

It is essential that every Lightworker take the time to walk the fine line between being both spiritually connected and physically grounded here on Earth. So do not take yourself for granted. You are the channel for light, and if the channel is not clear, the light will surely be blocked. Mind, body, and spirit must always remain free of any energetic clutter or baggage.

# 12

# Soul Contracts and the Nature of Relationships

The Beatles had a line on matters of the heart when they sang, "All you need is love...love is all you need." If only it were that simple! Love is so confusing, and it's no surprise that many of my clients, both male and female, seek me out with questions that pertain to matters of the heart. There are many people who don't feel complete if they don't have someone special in their life as a partner or a significant other. I know many who go on what is a lifetime quest to find their perfect person, or what is often called the "soulmate."

## Love Connections

Finding that person who connects on a soul level happens more than one would imagine; but deciphering the true meaning of the connection is the tricky part. The term "soul groups" pertains to many spirits who travel around in the same circles during different incarnations (or lifetimes). This indicates that we have many "soulmates" for many different reasons, who love and support us for all eternity. The nature of these soulmate relationships changes from one lifetime to the next, as we try to balance the scales of our karma and expand our light quotient. In one lifetime, two souls may have been husband and wife, in another perhaps mother and son, but then maybe the roles reverse. The scenarios could go on and on, repeating until both souls have fulfilled their obligations to each other, and gained enough soul knowledge to rise to the next plane. Before entering the current lifetime; two souls will come together and enter into a "soul contract." Bob may say to Mary, "You protected and cared for me when I was sick, next I will protect and care for you." Mary agrees and so the contract is binding. When the contract is fulfilled and all is settled, they are able to move on, free of any soul obligations.

## Sign on the Dotted Line

Just like contracts in business, the unexpected can always occur. Not everyone may uphold his or her end or he or she may break the deal. This leaves him or her indebted, and he or she is destined to repeat it next time around until the contract is fulfilled. Because the universe is always in perfect balance, it won't allow debts to go unpaid. It's like the annoying debt collector who calls and calls until you pay up! The universe will continue to throw this contract (or promise) that you made back at you until you uphold your end of the deal; this pertains to matters of the heart as well. My grandmother used to say in Italian, "God has slow feet, but he gets there in due time." In other words, everyone gets what he or she is owed eventually. She was so right.

### Read the Fine Print

When you sign a contract or make any agreement, it's important to know the details of what you're getting into. Now where confusion can come in with regard to soul circles, soul contracts, and marriage relationships is that one or more persons involved do not accept or have an awareness of the terms of the contract. Not all soul contracts are marriage contracts or meant to be binding for the remainder of the incarnation. Some people, just like ships that pass in the night, simply need to move through, fulfill their obligations and move on. Understanding that soul contracts have terms that will help you move on to a more enlightened existence when the time comes.

## We Meet Again

It has happened to all of us; you meet that guy or gal and are immediately swept off your feet. Although it could appear to feel like love at first sight, what it is in actuality is the soul memory being jarred and recognizing the person with whom you contracted before you entered this lifetime. Keep in mind, you have been here before and are bound to recognize the spirit with which you had an experience in a past life. Just like déjà vu, we experience a sense of familiarity that gives us the feeling of "Oh, we meet again."

## A Past-Life Connection

When I met my husband Steve, it was love at first sight for both of us. It was not until six months after we met that I remembered a past-life regression that I'd had about six years earlier. In the regression, I could see a small Japanese village. I was in a tiny hut with my husband and three children. I saw my husband's face clearly, and he looked like someone I knew or had known, yet had no idea from where. I knew that we were going to be overtaken by the samurai of a rival village, and that the children and I would be taken away and my husband would be killed. As our small village was being pillaged, the children and I huddled together in terror. I knew that I did not want to leave my husband and that he was being dishonored in some way. There was no way that he could protect us, and I saw the pain in his eyes as he knew that his family would be ripped away from him and that we would never be together again. Instead of being taken away from my husband, I saw a flash, and somehow my children lay still on the ground. I was not shown what actually happened, but I knew that I had somehow plunged a knife into my own stomach and killed myself.

As I awoke from the regression, in the present time, I felt the pain of losing my husband and my children. I found the regression scary and so sad. I was not sure why I was being shown this horrific scene. For years, I put it out of my mind until I realized; Steve was the man whom I had seen as my husband in the regression! The man who was so devastated to lose his family came back to make it right. His spirit needed to seek out and reunite his family once again; his soul was driven to fulfill his obligation to his family. It is no accident that Steve is half Asian and his grandfather is Japanese.

## Should I Stay or Should I Go?

I get calls from clients who are in absolutely miserable situations; troublesome relationships that are filled with jealousy, deceit, sometimes even abuse, yet they have difficulty letting them go. Many Lightworkers will stay in or even seek out dysfunctional relationships.

There are several reasons Lightworkers continually find themselves in unhappy relationships. For a Lightworker with heightened sensitivities, life can become a vicious cycle of highs and lows in an attempt to quell the anxieties that go along with the extrasensory perceptions. When we enter into a new romance, we become intoxicated by the feelings that it brings. Hormones and other chemical changes actually make us love drunk. But when reality sets in, the high that it brings will eventually bring on drastic lows. The Lightworker will become addicted to the feelings that a new romance brings, and seek it out over and over again. These highs will only temporarily soothe the suffering that the unaware Lightworker may be going through. Ultimately, it will only bring more pain when we reap the consequences of rushing into consecutive bad relationships to quell the misplaced emotions that we experience from our own heightened components.

Also, another problem that Lightworkers face is that they are caretakers. As strong Empaths, they will not only continuously draw wounded people to them, but literally seek them out. Eventually, the Lightworker becomes drained and depleted from trying to heal everyone, and feelings of being used and foolish take over, finally leaving the Lightworker wondering when he or she will be loved for who he or she is and not for being there to "fix" everyone. Just like the bright light bulb on our front porch, the Lightworker's bright light draws a lot of bugs! Realizing what you are and controlling your heightened components will help you to not seek relief in the form of relationships. It is important to seek out relationships that are equitable and not one-sided. Remember that balance is very important to the Lightworker. Without it, Lightworkers become unfocused, disorientated, and miserable. So whenever you begin to feel that you are giving too much, you most likely are becoming drained of your light energy, and it is time to either balance out the scales in your relationships or walk away.

## Little Miss Fix-It

My long-term client Karen, an advertising executive from Toronto and unaware Lightworker, met a man called Gary through a mutual friend. She would call and tell me how they just clicked right off the bat and that the chemistry between them was magnetic. This went on for several months, and everything appeared to be going well. I would counsel her periodically if she was feeling insecure or misunderstood in the relationship.

Karen had always been a confident and self-reliant woman, but at times, Gary was making her feel insecure or just not good enough. About six months into the relationship, things seemed to take a turn for the worse. Gary began to become jealous, possessive, and controlling. Karen would call and tell me that she loved him, but felt that Gary was now overbearing and controlling. It turned out that Gary had been through a painful divorce and his ex-wife had cheated on him. His ego, pride, and self-esteem were wounded, and he was desperately looking to Karen to resolve his issues. Gary was drawn to Karen because of her healing Lightworker energy, and Karen was drawn to Gary because he was wounded and her inner Lightworker was always seeking to heal someone.

Karen soon realized that no matter what she did, she could not heal Gary's wounds and that he needed to do this himself. She did not want to end the relationship; but she was beginning to feel that it was not enhancing her life, but rather becoming a drain on her. Ultimately, she decided to end the relationship because the imbalance that it was creating was affecting her entire life. I supported her decision and helped her through the process of grieving the breakup. It was important for Karen to realize that she was acting in more of a Lightworker capacity, trying to heal Gary.

A relationship should not involve you trying to fix or heal a wounded partner; it should be an equitable exchange of love and support. In this case, I did support Karen; but my suggestions on a relationship usually depend on the depth of the relationship. For example, if the individuals are in a troubled romance (such as Karen and Gary), I may advise them to move on and offer support in the process. If they have taken the relationship to a point at which their lives are so entwined that there is no immediate release (children, financial commitments), I may make other suggestions. I knew from Karen's readings that she had contracted with another soul for marriage and children. The longer she procrastinated about the relationship with Gary, the longer she delayed her marriage partner from coming into her life. This was her free will. The man whom she was meant to marry would have to wait until she accepted the fact that she could not heal Gary and had to let him go.

## How Do We Know When to Let Go?

This is a question that I get all the time. The answer is, we usually get many signs, (remember your Lightworker gift of awareness) although we refuse to see them. If we honestly look at our situation, we can see that we are beating a dead horse and know when it's time to say goodbye. We have many tools to guide us on the roads that we choose. Using your Lightworker gifts as a guide can help you through the obstacle courses of your relationships. We need to recognize the differences between relationships; which ones we need to stay in versus the ones that are a result of either being an unaware Lightworker or a partner in a soul contract. Each one could feel like euphoria, each one could break your heart, and both are meant for the purpose of spiritual progress. This is how the two can compare to each other:

| **Soul Contract or Unaware Lightworker Relationship** | **Life Partnership** |
|---|---|
| Could feel like love at first sight. | Could feel like love at first sight. |
| Could have a lot of passion for a certain time span. | Could have a lot of passion for a certain time span. |
| The relationship could be happy for a short time. | The relationship becomes stabilized. |
| The relationship could become codependent. | The relationship is equitable. |
| The relationship could become violent. | Your life is enriched. |
| The relationship makes you feel depressed. | You feel contentment. |
| The relationship makes you feel drained. | You feel secure. |
| The relationship brings you frustration. | You care for your partner when he or she is in need. |
| The relationship stops you from achieving your truc goals. | Your partner cares for you when you are in need. |
| There could be jealousy and deceit in the relationship. | You support each other in manifesting your individual dreams. |
| You feel like your partner does not respect you. | You work to build a life together, not destroy each other's lives individually. You feel complete. (Jerry McGuire was right on point.) |
| You feel misunderstood. | |
| You feel like you need to get out. | |

As you can see, they start off the same way, but end up very differently. Now the ideal situation is to realize what type of relationship you are in early on before any damage is done, or you dig a hole that you cannot get out of. If we are really honest with ourselves, it can be very easy to distinguish between the two types of relationships.

## How Our Ego Gets in the Way

Our spirit knows our true path. The soul always knows its path and will do anything to follow it. The spirit has to battle another powerful force—our ego. This is what keeps us trapped in these life-lesson relationships, and prevents us from manifesting what we really desire. The ego, wounded and fear-based, will gather up all our life experiences, hurts, pains, or insecurities, and throw them out at us at the most inopportune times. For example, it's true that most of us feel pushed by our egos to have a life partner, and we'll stretch the truth in order to find one.

Jenna was a 40-year-old lawyer who called me for a reading. She was dating a man at work who was married, but he was certainly going to leave his wife for her because that's what he had been promising for the last year. "Why are you doing this to yourself?" I asked her. "Do you really want a man in your life that has a wife and children? Do you even really want a relationship?"

The truth was that Jenna's parents divorced when she was young, and she was scared to death of love. On a deeper level, she spent most of her adult life choosing men who had issues that were so complicated that a relationship with Jenna wasn't in the cards. As a lawyer, Jenna was used to going up against tough adversaries in court. If another woman such as a wife was in the picture, Jenna's ego dictated that she would "win" the guy away. We had to take her issues down to a spiritual level to figure out why she was abusing herself in this way. Before she even told me about her parents' rocky marriage, I sat her down for a reading and the answers were obvious to me.

* * * *

"I see a father. He is walking out the door instead of in the door," I said.

"I see a mother who is crying," I continued.

At that point, I knew the depth of Jenna's pain and could feel her life-long torment of believing that men don't stay, but look for the quickest escape route possible.

It followed that Jenna chose unavailable men because she knew on a psychic level that they would never really walk in the door with both feet. This way, they could never really hurt her on the deepest level, because she knew that the love would be fleeting from the start.

I did a reading with a woman named Lydia who didn't say anything, but simply sat down on my couch and told me that she was feeling depressed. "You have issues with your father," I said. "I've never met my father," she said. "He left before I was born." "And now another man has left you and that's why you're here," I said.

Her deep-rooted abandonment issues had come to the forefront again when her husband of 10 years announced that he wanted a divorce and had a new girlfriend.

"Lydia, what you don't consciously realize is that you came into this world with abandonment issues," I said. "Your spirit came here wounded, knowing that part of your life would be missing."Lydia's mother loved her; but on a spiritual level, she grew up with a serious fear of men and their intentions. The interesting part of our reading was the fact that her husband walking out seemed expected. Her issues with her father remained unhealed.

"I didn't realize until now how much I really miss my father, which seems strange because I never met him," she said. "I guess before I go on in life, I need to deal with these issues." It's hard to say this because what Lydia's husband did by cheating was heinous; but some of the blame was the result of his wife's torments. "I guess I pulled away from my husband emotionally in the second year of our marriage," she said. "Deep down, I still feel like I'll never really be happy in a close male-female relationship, so spiritually I pulled out and detached before he could detach and leave." It was almost a self-fulfilling wish. She took her loving energy out of the relationship and her husband felt abandoned. It took many years, but after hanging in there and waiting for his wife to return to him, he decided that it was impossible and looked for love elsewhere. Lydia had literally turned him into her father.

Now if Lydia could peel back all the layers of her ego and get down to her true spiritual self, she would be able to find her way. The ego loves to throw out these roadblocks to our happiness, especially in relationships. We need to find the tools to toss them aside and listen to our spiritual selves instead of our wounded egos. The key here is to use your heightened components, especially the gift of awareness, and keep your eyes open for signs. If we truly listened to the guidance and direction that is always there for us, we could find our way to our life partner.

## Build a Mate

If only you could go to a one-stop-soulmate store and punch in a few particulars. You might write, "I'm looking for someone tall, dark, handsome, good sense of humor, and likes Adam Sandler movies. Oh, he also has to love kids and cats." There are dating services that promise that if you just answer a complicated set of questions, they will put your answers through a computer and out will pop your soulmate. He might live in Alaska while you dwell in New Jersey, but the good news is, he's out there standing on some snow-capped mountain waiting just for you. And he likes cats.

## Ghosts of Relationships Past

When you find love, the confusion becomes thicker, and emotions can even get murkier, because many times your past experiences with relationships will influence your current one. These are soul wounds that you have not healed. We need to heal the wounds of our past or they will continually cause us pain.

If a past partner cheated on you, then a surge of jealousy might feel overwhelming when your new person talks to the supermarket checkout girl. Maybe you've never had really great self-esteem and can't believe that someone would love you. Unconsciously, you do almost everything possible to derail the new relationship, including pulling back on your emotions in order to protect your heart from future hurt. I had a client who was deeply in love with a man who lived around the corner from her Detroit home. After years of talking, friendship, and even a bit of flirting, he finally confessed to the fact that he loved her...and had for years. They dated for a blissful summer until she decided to suddenly dump him. He couldn't understand what had happened and thought that perhaps he didn't have a nice enough home or car for her tastes. That wasn't even the least bit true. She pulled out, figuring that she would beat him to the punch because nothing this beautiful could last forever.

## Releasing Your Ghosts

We have all been left injured by romantic relationships at one time or another. How do we heal these wounds in order to become healthy enough to embark upon another relationship? Carrying the dark energy of a dysfunctional relationship will surely infect the next one. It is a necessity to heal and cleanse the ego and spirit before moving on. Perhaps you know someone who is beautiful, successful, and fun, yet he or she can never seem to find a great romantic partner; and if he or she does find one, the relationship doesn't last very long. One of the reasons, if you look at this from a spiritual standpoint, is that he or she truly has mistaken the nature of the connection.

I believe that the universe does have a soulmate or many soulmates designed for your current life. That doesn't mean that others won't enter your life on a romantic level, but these relationships will be fleeting because this person isn't there to give you what you ultimately need or want. In other words, it's simple; this isn't the one who you're supposed to be with in this life.

I have many clients who are like Mary, a 30-year-old teacher who is very relationship savvy, but confused by her current breakup. It seemed that Tim was perfect for her. He was a CPA with a promising future. They dated for a year, went on a few vacations together, and even met each other's families. But there seemed to be an invisible wall where Tim wouldn't really discuss a real future, and Mary was nervous about bringing it up. When he finally confessed that he loved her, but wasn't "in love" with her and wanted to see other people, she was devastated. Then she made an appointment with me.

"But I love him," she told me through her tears. "I thought that he was going to ask me to be his wife." We dug a little deeper and I found out that Mary wanted to get to the "finish line" with Tim and get the ring, the house, and the family, but when she really stopped for a moment to consider if Tim was "the one" she had to pause. "He has a great job and nice family," she said. "It makes sense." It made sense to me that Mary was like many single women who didn't want to throw away someone who seemed like a sensible choice. There were so many times in life where there wasn't even that type of choice available in a sea of men that made Tim look like a prince. But just because someone looks "good on paper" or seems like a reasonable choice doesn't mean that on a spiritual level he or she is our life mate. You really have to cull it down to the real person. Ask your heart and dig into your soul to answer this question: is this person my spiritual partner on the deepest level?

It's true that most of us feel the need to have a life partner, and we'll stretch the truth in order to find one. Going back to my client Lydia, we can see that she went into her relationship almost manifesting the guy to leave her through her thinking and feelings of deep insecurity. She never felt satisfied because of an event that happened before she was even born. Now that Lydia knew her issues from our reading, and her awareness of the deep-seated insecurities were right in her face, she could begin to tackle her demons.

She could heal. She could love again someday without putting the abandonment blanket on every man whom she would ever meet again in her life. In fact, a funny thing happened to her after doing some work with her counselor and me.

Two years later, after her divorce was final, she met a single dad at her daughter's school bake sale. He was fumbling with a tray of cupcakes that she helped to arrange despite the horrible messy frosting that had been the result of a harried parent trying to do 10 million things at the same time. It turns out that his wife had died three years earlier. Both were a little afraid of love and decided to become friends. Two years later, they were married. This information tells us that the recipe to manifesting a life partnership (or marriage) is not simple, but can be done if we recognize certain clues that are really very apparent. In relationships, remember to always use your Lightworker gifts of:

- Intuition.
- Sensitivity.
- Awareness.
- Empathy.
- Belief.

Also keep in mind that not all love connections are meant to be marriage commitments, but can also be deeply spiritual in nature. If we truly accept the nature of our relationships, are in a relationship for the right reasons, and use our components as our guides, we will progress to the next step on our path, ultimately leading to a happy life and a fulfilling relationship.

Each person who comes into your life has a purpose. Live, learn, love, and remember, no connection with another's spirit is ever in vain.

# Part IV:

# Death Is Just a Door

# 13

# Spirit, the Journeyman, and the Mortal Apprenticeship

As we have discussed, our spiritual selves are journeymen constantly on a quest for enlightenment, spiritual purity, an expansion of our light energy. Even as Lightworkers, as we journey through our own spiritual path, the ultimate goal is to harbor more unconditional love, light, and wisdom within our energetic selves. As we move forward, it is helpful to have a conscious awareness of a big picture. It is vital to keep in mind that this lifetime is just a small piece of the mosaic that is your eternal self. Understanding the power of now, what is happening in your life and how it will affect you later will allow you to plan for your spiritual future in this lifetime and other lifetimes to come. Living with the notion that we have been here before and will probably return again someday changes our perspective on life. As spirits, we are eternal journeymen; in mortal form, we are apprentices on the journey.

As we experience Earth life, we are expected to expand our light by overcoming lessons and challenges that will allow us to rise up. We often wonder why we are faced with difficulties and hardships, but it's not about the situations that we must endure. It's about how we endure them with love and pure intentions, each day, learning how to learn to live in a place of gratitude, and blessing the process of learning, as painful as it may be, or sinking deeper and deeper into the dark energy that envelopes us during these times. For each hardship that we rise above, we expand our light and that of the collective. This is all a part of gathering the soul knowledge that we need to move to the next level of our journey. Each lifetime or apprenticeship is a chance to be closer to a glorious place of love, light, and wisdom.

Within our soul is a history rich with knowledge and experience. It is buried deep within our being, but it is there each day for us to access. We carry our soul knowledge with us from one lifetime to the next. What we acquire is never lost; we enter into this world holding all the information that our soul has gathered along the way, prepared to learn even more. Many of us just "know" things and do not understand how we know; this is the soul memory reminding us of something that we have already learned. Past-life experiences, traumas, triumphs are carried with us. As we've discussed, the love that we feel for others is carried with us as well. Not one shred of wisdom, hardship, or love is ever lost or wasted along the soul's journey.

Experiences on the Earth plane and beyond are forever a part of the fabric of our soul, a tapestry so intertwined with the collective that the place where our spirit ends and the universe begins seems blurred. This is why we can literally see the wisdom of the ages when we look into a newborn's eyes.

## The Journey of Transitioning

There comes a time when our mortal apprenticeship is complete, and our basket is full from all the fruits of our labors here on Earth. The spirit slowly begins to break away from the body. Because the physical body is fueled by the energetic self or soul, it begins the process of breaking down. This usually manifests as what we know as illness or old age. The transition does not happen as suddenly as you may think. It could take years, months or weeks, depending on how quickly the spirit wants to pull out of the physical experience; but it is a decision that souls make to exit at a certain time. Their learning is complete, and they are prepared to move on with their journey. For those of us who have not gathered enough knowledge to leave this apprenticeship, it can be difficult and painful to understand the transition process.

### It's Hard to Say Good-Bye

I'll never forget the young husband who lost his pregnant wife in a tragic car accident. The shock and grief of what occurred was so strong that he found it hard to carry on living. He began to skip work and not pay his bills anymore. After he lost his wife and child, his life began to spiral out of control as his grief took over his very existence. He was tormented that he never got to see the birth of his son and worried that his wife and child had suffered in their last moments. He told me that he came to me "as a last resort." We sat down and immediately I began to feel the presence of his young wife who so died tragically.

She appeared to me holding an infant child in a blue blanket. She smiled and nodded her head as if to reassure him that they both had arrived safely in the spirit world. She then began to urge him to go on and remember the promise he made to her. When I relayed the message a look of disbelief came over his face. As it turns out, he explained to me when she was lying in a hospital bed during her last days, he whispered a promise in her ear that he would never forget her and they would be a family again one day in heaven. When she reminded him of the promise, he knew he would make good on it because now he was sure that his wife and child were waiting for him to be reunited one day. He was able to say goodbye that day and finally felt some closure. He went to work the next day and slowly the pieces of his life began to click into place again.

When a loved one transitions into the spirit world, we always wonder why. We feel betrayed by God, and by our loved one. We may deny or refuse to accept it; we may internalize our pain and feel incomplete. There seems to be no answers, no one to blame, and we finally come to the realization (however way we can) that life here on Earth has to go on and we are left with no choice but to turn our focus in another direction and carry on with our own journey. Rarely do we consider the transitioning spirit to be the master of his/her own destiny and celebrate his/her choice to move on. Because we are all masters of our own journey, *we* make the choice of when to leave the Earth plane. When our apprenticeship is complete, we are free, released from the constraint of our physical bodies and free to view the Earth plane without ourselves in it. With your apprenticeship completed, you are granted license to move forward. Suffering and sickness become tiresome and a spirit who longs for freedom makes the brave choice to go. When the spirit has expanded its light enough, he or she is ready to move on to the next phase of the journey. It is not the end; it is a new beginning. Death is just a door.

14

# The Medium: Our Link to Those Who have Traveled On

A medium is a person who can communicate with those who have crossed over into the spirit world. Their function is to be the links between two worlds. Our loved ones who cross over never go far—usually in the Astral plane—and communication is always possible. Mediums are psychics who can talk to the dead, but the psychic reader and the medium are not the same. The distinct difference between the two is that they extract information from two separate sources. The psychic extracts information from Source intelligence, and the medium must actually dialogue with the essence of a spirit, the ethereal or energetic self of the person who passed on.

The spirit engaged in communication may be well-adjusted and able to communicate, or may be confused, scared, and caught in a world between worlds. The medium has the difficult task of translating communication that may not always be clearly understood. The purpose of mediumship is to heal both the spirit and the person in the physical, and this must be done with care, concern, and caution. This spirit has not crossed over and suddenly become all-knowing and psychic. In fact, he or she crossed over with the same personality as he or she had when he or she was in the physical. Don't expect Uncle Frank who passed away to start telling you your future, and don't be shocked when Uncle Frank makes the same jokes that you heard every year at the family's Thanksgiving table. In fact, that bad joke is evidential proof that we are indeed communicating with Uncle Frank!

It may be true that Uncle Frank can see a little more than we can here in the physical, and also see things from a different perspective; but he does not become this profound being right away. The essence of Uncle Frank is still the Uncle Frank you knew. Uncle Frank can always progress and grow in the spirit world, but will always retain what you always knew and loved about him. My client Bob lost his good friend Gil who passed away at age 50 from a heart attack. Gil was a long-time practical joker who loved to "pull one over" on his good friends. After Gil's passing, Bob couldn't believe the moments in his life where little jokes seemed to be played on him with no one "there" on the other end doing it. Then Bob would chuckle and think of one person—Gil. Even on the other side, his friend still had a wicked sense of humor!

## The Lightworker's Clear Channel

Lightworkers have a natural inclination to mediumship, because Lightworkers are descended from the higher realms, and their channel is clear and illuminated for communication. Many Lightworkers experience spontaneous communication and may not understand what is happening. If you have ever spoken to a deceased loved one in a dream, smelled his or her perfume or heard his or her voice in your head, you have spontaneously used your mediumship gifts. This can be a wonderful thing or can be troublesome to the unaware Lightworker who is bothered or pestered by uninvited communication from the other side. The latter can be avoided with some simple practices.

### Set Your Intentions High

When practicing your mediumship, it is important that the intention is to heal and enlighten all parties involved. Mediumship is not a parlor trick or ego booster. There are many ways to open up communication with the dead, but all must be done with the intention of the greatest good of all. Let's examine one method, the Ouija board. There is nothing evil about the Ouija board; it is merely a tool or focal point for mediumship. The Ouija board is only another way to facilitate communication and can be a useful tool in contacting the dead. Yet, there is fear and stigma associated with the board. Since the early 1960s, it has been sold as a "game." Children or people with the wrong intentions got their hands on the planchette and attracted spirits with the same misguided intentions. If you decide to use a Ouija board, it is important to bless the process and shield yourself before you begin. People who do not shield themselves before they begin, and make light of any channeling method, will invoke spirits who want to play games, frighten or, even worse, attach themselves to the earthly beings who called on them in the first place.

## Stay Balanced

The quality and level of communication can very much depend on the emotional state of the mediums themselves. If you are going to communicate with the other side, it is important that you are balanced and free of any emotional issues that may make you a target of an unscrupulous spirit. A Lightworker whose emotional state is shaky can invoke spirits who want to control, manipulate, or frighten. Remember your general state of being transmutes your energy field, and when your energy field has excess darkness, it is best to put the communication on hold or you will be at risk of attracting spirits with dark energy as well.

Carolyn was studying metaphysics and mediumship. Carolyn had some emotional issues and suffered from untreated obsessive compulsive disorder. She began using the Ouija board with her husband for daily guidance. Her husband, who had a history of depression and substance abuse, was now in recovery and seeking enlightenment as well. The two began to use the board on a daily basis for insight, but quickly became addicted to the communication. They spoke with the same spirit each day, and developed a sense of trust and confidence in the spirit. Then one day, the spirit on the board proclaimed itself to be Jesus Christ and told them that they had to get out of their home because Satan was coming to find them there. Carolyn and her husband were people who had some personal issues and were vulnerable. The spirit found that he could control and frighten the couple and sent them on a week-long road trip from New Jersey to Florida, running for their lives from Satan.

"Don't stay at the Holiday Inn, Satan is in there!" the spirit warned.

"Don't go into that diner, he is in there sitting at the counter waiting for you."

They panicked and drove in circles, listening to this controlling and mischievous spirit that was preying on their fears. Finally, Carolyn called me from Florida to ask my advice "Jesus is on the Ouija board, and he said my niece's black kitten must be destroyed because Satan has possessed it. Then we can return home."

"Hold on now!" I told her. "Use your common sense. Do you think Jesus Christ would come on to the board and tell you to kill an innocent kitten?"

After a long discussion, I was able to convince them to toss the board out and begin the long drive back to New Jersey. It was a frightening experience for the couple and left them shaken and distressed.

This is just one example of the kind of horrible results that can occur when people who are not emotionally stable practice mediumship. Mediumship is meant to enlighten and heal, never to destroy. Your general state of being and the amount of dark energy in your own energy field will affect the quality of the spirits you attract. Carolyn and her husband still had some personal issues to work on before they should ever have attempted to communicate with the spirit world.

## Develop Your Craft

I had my first experience with mediumship at the age of three when the spirit of my deceased uncle came to me in a very gentle and playful way. Children have the natural propensity of seeing beyond the physical because they are so unaffected and open-minded. Talking to him seemed as natural as breathing.

"Tell your mother that I love her," he said.

"I will," I promised. "Please come visit me again."

And he did several times when I was a little girl, popping into my room in the wee hours to let us know that he was happy on the other side, but still was with us at all times. It was an early lesson for me when it came to not fearing death, but knowing that it was just another passage for our spirits. To me, as a child, this all came very naturally and seemed like nothing unusual. Many children with imaginary friends could very well be communicating with loved ones who have passed on.

As I got older, I began to think that hearing voices crying out for help in the night was not exactly "normal." The voices would come with messages or just to make it known that they were with me. After a while, I considered these nightly visitors part of my routine. I'd close my eyes and sometimes wait to hear them, and I was disappointed on nights when I drifted off to sleep alone.

Some of us are born with a natural inclination to mediumship, while others are called to it later in life and work to develop it. Whether you are a born medium or you work at it, you, as the instrument for the spirit, need to constantly exercise your gift. You cannot stop learning and it is a skill that gets better with practice. Still, there are so many mediums out there professing to talk to the dead as easily as talking on a telephone, just like the cell phone commercial that says "Can you hear me now?"

## Evidential Mediumship

I've seen mediums face a large audience that includes people who are over 60. The medium will ask if someone lost a grandmother or aunt who went by the name of Rose. Now, that was a very popular name six decades ago and inevitably many hands will be lifted in the air. The medium will say that he or she can call up all the Roses at will, which is rarely the case. By the way, be careful if the medium asks if Rose died in a sudden way. These generic questions are easy ones and these types of readings should be approached with some caution. A true medium will get down to specifics and not speak in broad generalities.

I prefer a medium who can bring to life the loved one on the other side with names, personality traits, and clear messages.

The true medium can link to the person in spirit and bring evidential proof that he or she is indeed talking to who the spirit claims to be. Mediumship is serious business and requires training in specific techniques to bring the evidence through clearly. A born medium or not, there is never enough training or practice. The more you work on it, the better you get. I know a medium that at 20 was naturally very gifted and could give certain messages and personality traits. As she worked at enhancing her gift, she could reveal so much more in terms of details. Again, it's all about embracing your mediumship, finding what works best for you, and then developing it.

## The Trance Medium

There are two main types of mediums. I'll start with trance or physical mediums. This is when the spirit actually enters the body of the medium and conveys his/her message. This can be done in a group setting or private meeting. Many people even report seeing the medium's features actually transform and begin to look like the spirit that he or she is channeling. The people in the room can listen as the spirit speaks through the medium, but the medium has no or very limited memory of what was said. Author Jane Roberts practiced this in her "Seth material." Seth is a spiritual teacher from the higher realms who spoke through Jane while she was in trance. Seth's empowering messages literally launched the new age movement in the 1960s, and Jane wrote many books from this knowledge.

## The Mental Medium

This is when the medium is fully aware of his/her surroundings and messages come through telepathically or through any number of ways, such as seeing pictures, hearing voices, or even physically feeling what the spirit is trying to communicate. I've conducted many readings where I can see a spirit enter a room and then it will communicate his or her wishes. Then, there are also times when I can only feel the spirit, but that doesn't mean that the spirit is any less powerful a presence. The mental medium uses any of the *clair* skills to communicate—clairvoyance (clear seeing), clairaudience (clear hearing), and so on.

## Healing Words

A mediumship reading is a profound healing experience. When a grieving loved one comes in for a reading and communicates, the grieving process can be accelerated tremendously. A truly evidential mediumship reading that reunites a grief-stricken person with his or her loved one can immediately transmute the dark energy of grief and begin to turn it into light. As the Lightworker medium, you have to come prepared to deliver a life-altering experience, so bring at least one box of tissues. The tears will surely flow, and the pain is soothed by the messages delivered through you from those in the spiritworld. It is an honor, privilege, and a huge responsibility to be the channel for those on the other side.

## How Long Do We Have to Wait?

Although we may be anxious to connect with a loved one whom we have recently lost, sometimes it is not possible. Sometimes a spirit is not ready to communicate. For example, if someone crossed over in a traumatic way, or in severe pain, there may be a period of convalescence and adjustment. Be assured that loved ones are there with these types of spirits to help them in their transition process. Once a spirit is fully and comfortably transitioned, he or she is usually ready and able to come through and welcome the chance to tell his or her grieving loved ones that he or she is just fine and still exists. Grieving loved ones can keep a spirit Earth-bound in an attempt to console those who they left behind. Many spirits do not want to carry on with their journey without making sure that their loved ones are okay. This is how a psychic medium can be of assistance to both the spirit and the ones left behind who are grieving—by delivering messages of evidential proof that their loved one has survived death.

## It's a Partnership

As a medium, you are in partnership with those in the spirit world. I have watched many mediums totally screw up a message, and I can actually feel the spirit as he or she is pulling his or her esoteric hairs out in frustration. I usually don't like to interrupt a medium who is delivering a message, but sometimes I feel compelled. Inside I am screaming (along with the deceased). "No!" Imagine the frustration of trying to give a message and your translator gets it all wrong? At that point, even the spirit is having an exasperated moment. Let's say a spirit has decided to return to give a loved one a special message or even a warning. If the medium can't quite get that message right, then the spirit will certainly have to work harder in order to make up for the deficiencies of the medium. This can be frustrating for all parties. Just like the psychic reader, the medium has an ego and the messages have to filter through. If the filter is not clear, it distorts the messages. This is why it is so important to keep your humility while you practice your lightwork. If your ego gets too big, it will totally defeat the purpose of your role here on Earth. Remember you are just a humble messenger.

## A Special Language All Your Own

Being a good medium means creating a language all your own for spirits to communicate with you. This language consists of symbolisms, memories, feelings, or any number of images that you have stored in your own memory bank. Because you are the instrument for the spirit, he or she must work within your frame of reference in order for you to comprehend the messages. Because these spirits no longer speak our language and are communicating energetically (although words will come through, words are the medium's frame of reference), they must communicate within the boundaries of the instrument (the medium) that they are utilizing.

They want to communicate with us as much as we want to communicate with them, so they will work with us any way that they can. For example, if I get a spirit who on Earth spoke only Japanese and wanted to show me Japanese symbols or words, we would have to figure out something because unfortunately, the Japanese language is not in my knowledge pool. Therefore, to be able to get the messages correctly, the medium should create a system to interpret the messages coming through.

For example, if I am communicating with someone's grandmother on the maternal side of the family, I will see a picture of my maternal grandmother. If I were to get a glimpse of a random elderly woman, I may be able to identify her as a grandmother, but by going into my own memory bank and extracting an image, I am able to specify the side of the family from which this grandmother is coming.

As a medium, you should establish your own personal symbols to help you to translate spirit messages as specifically as possible. Many mediums will use left side for father and right side for mother; but because I am dyslexic, I have difficulty with left and right! So again, the spirit is willing to work with me, and show me specific pictures that are already stored in my memory bank. Then there are times when the spirit will show me specific scenes from my childhood. I may see a scene from our family picnic when I was about 10 years old. I will then have to tell the sitter (the one sitting in front of me); "Your Uncle Frank wants me to mention a family picnic?" I may also give specific details of what I am seeing and the sitter will understand the message.

Because we all have different content in our memory banks, when practicing your mediumship, you should develop your own system of identifiers for communication to pull out specific information. You can use images, words, scents, or feelings that reflect experiences in your own life, and then relay them to the sitter who will piece them together from there.

## Establish a Relationship With Your "Gatekeeper"

Many times, there is more than one deceased loved one coming through. I remember a reading where a mother lost grown twin sons in a boating accident. She was closer to the son named Jeremy and estranged from the one named Josh. During our reading, she was hoping to just connect with Jeremy and was shocked when Josh also appeared to tell his mother that he was sorry about the meaningless fighting that they'd had when he was alive. Eventually, both sons were there at our reading, which was the best present this mother could receive. Often, there could be a whole group on the other side just waiting their turn to give a message or just say hello. Because we don't want to open the floodgates and have everyone talking at once, mediums have what they call a "gatekeeper" to help them to keep the spirits in line. This is a spirit guide who is assigned to you specifically for the purpose of your mediumship work. Think of him as the guy who keeps everyone in line at Disneyworld! Remember Whoopi Goldberg in *Ghost*? Obviously, she was not using her gatekeeper when her room was overwhelmed with spirits trying to talk, and she said, "We got spooks coming in from Jersey here!"

Your gatekeeper will also identify and bring through the strongest communicator of the group. Some spirits (just like any of us) have better communication skills than others. We may as well use our time wisely and bring through the spirit who is able to convey his or her message most clearly. If you don't use a gatekeeper, you can be flooded with messages and quickly become confused. Think of your gatekeeper as part of your spiritual entourage of guides and teachers in the spirit-world who help you with your work here on Earth. Again, it's really important to work with and establish a relationship with a gatekeeper when you begin the practice of mediumship.

## How to Open Up a Dialogue

Once you have shielded and set your intentions, you can begin to link to the spirit world. At this time, you should also have established your personal indicators to translate spirit messages, as well as a gatekeeper by your side. Opening dialogue is easy if we start with some basic questions. I like to begin a basic question and answer session in my head. Using this process of question and answer can keep everything in order and be less confusing for the medium. The medium must keep control of the session at all times. Otherwise, it would be like a translator at the U.N. trying to translate for ten different leaders who are all yelling out random messages without being asked. Whew! My head hurts just thinking about it.

## Who's That Knocking at My Door?

You want to identify who is coming through first. Does the energy feel feminine? Is it maternal or nurturing? Then it is possible that you have someone's mother or grandmother. Is the energy masculine, authoritative, or paternal? Then you may have a father energy present. Next, you will usually receive an identifying symbol. A flash of your father's face may come to mind, or you may smell his cologne; any signal to identify to you that a father is coming through. At that point, you should relay to your client, "I have a gentleman here and he feels very paternal, perhaps a father figure." It is important to specify that this is a father *figure*, it could be someone who took the role as his or her father or a father-in-law. This doesn't have to be a biological relationship, and we cannot assume anything. The client will need more information now. Next question to the spirit: What was your cause of death? Break it down into five categories, and then go down the list until you feel a positive response:

- Natural causes (old age).
- Accident.
- Disease.
- Suicide.
- Murder.

At this time, quiet your mind and wait for the answer, and amazingly enough, the answer always comes. You may even begin to feel physical discomfort. For example, you may experience head pain if someone died of a traumatic head injury (category: accident). Then you can tell your sitter, "This man died in an accident, and my head is throbbing, indicating that he may have suffered a head injury."At this point, it will usually click, "Oh yes, my father was killed in a car accident when I was five." Now it is time to go further into the dialogue, asking the spirit specific questions regarding:

- Name.
- Age at death.
- Specific memories.
- Specific messages.

This is how we identify to whom we are speaking and the message that he or she wants to convey. You will find that if you keep this sequence, the messages will come in a very clear and organized manner, making it easier for you to relay the information.

## Oh...It's Him?

Your clients may not always get who they came to hear from. Our loved ones may not be available at any given time, and because many in the spirit world want to chit chat, anyone could stop by and say hi. For example, my client Silvia came to communicate with her beloved father and was elated when I told her that we had a father energy present when we opened up our session. As I began to describe personality traits and give more details, her face changed. "That doesn't sound like my father." I went deeper with more detail and then she gasped "That is my ex-father- in-law! I don't want to talk to him!" Well he wanted to talk to her that day, and that is who came through! Your sitter will not always get to communicate with who he or she came for, but I always tell him or her, you get what you get and don't get upset!

There are many ways to be able to identify who is trying to come through. You can also relay personality traits of the spirit to your clients by paying attention to how you are feeling during the reading. Do you feel agitated, jovial, stern, or sad? This is most likely an indicator of the spirit with whom you are linking.

I may say, "There is a gentleman here, and I am feeling very impatient, like he wants to get through and right away."

Then the sitter may say, "Yes, my ex-father-in-law was quite impatient and never liked to wait for anything."

## Don't Let the Tail Wag the Dog!

I remember one client who was in her 90s and wanted to talk to a group of ladies with whom she used to play cards when they were young mothers and housewives. We sat down and talked about a few particulars of her card games, but it didn't take more than a minute or two before the room was flooded with ladies rushing in to talk about their families, their love for each other, and who won that big tournament game back in 1962!

The point is that spirits can be persistent at times, but the medium should never allow those present on the other side to take over a session, or your life for that matter. Mediums who tell of spirits popping up in grocery stores and out of closets are not managing their mediumship gifts properly. Just because you have a gift to communicate with the dead does not mean you aren't entitled to have a life that is free of disruptions. As the instrument for communication, a medium must be protected and shielded in order to not become exhausted. If you are an instrument for spirit communication, treat yourself like a valuable instrument! It's the only way that you will have the stamina to keep up with your work. Those on the other side will wait if need be, although they'll "give it a good try" to get your attention.

I'll never forget Fred, who was a longtime suitor of a woman named Joyce. Fred wouldn't leave me alone around Valentine's Day because he simply needed to profess his love for Joyce one more time. Finally, during our reading, Joyce laughed when I told her about Fred and admitted that she always had a bit of a secret crush on him, too. That was all Fred needed to hear. He was at peace and Joyce was smiling. I took a deep breath and knew that we may be back in the same situation next Valentine's Day!

# 15

# The Earthbound: Lost Souls and the Accidental Tourist

In my many years as a medium, I have encountered many different types of spirits—some adjusted and happy in the nonphysical realms and some not so happy. When a spirit is unsettled in the spirit realm, the spirit tends to hang around on the Earth plane, becoming what we call an earthbound spirit. Often, earthbound spirits attach to humans (although the people they attach to don't always understand what's going on), causing a variety of problems.

If a spirit attaches to you, that attachment can drain your energy (not unlike a house guest who won't leave), causing you to feel tired and weak. You may get headaches and have trouble sleeping. You might feel anxious or depressed, or you could suffer from bouts of anger or any number of other issues caused by this psychic drain.

Don't confuse this with haunting or a possession, by the way. It's not the same thing. These earthbound spirits are merely lost and confused—they're not ghosts who haunt (which happens when spirits refuse to leave and become deliberately mischievous and antagonistic), nor are they demons (entities comprised of pure evil that never take human form).

Many reasons exist for why a spirit remains earthbound, including still feeling the pull of addictions, a desire to help grieving loved ones, being very attached to a home or other physical location, or refusing to accept that he or she is dead—often because the person had died suddenly or unexpectedly, never having a chance to psychologically prepare himself or herself for the transition. Unfinished business with others still alive or even a lack of belief in life after death can also keep a spirit earthbound.

When spirits are earthbound, their personal crisis becomes a problem for all of us because of the effect they have on the planet's energy. During our time here on Earth, each of us creates our own energy field. If we live in a in a way that expands unconditional love and increases light, we harbor more light energy. If we live in a state of negativity because of attachments and emotional situations that are unhealthy, then we harbor more dark energy. Wherever we are on the light or dark spectrum, this energy is our true essence—our spiritual self.

When we cross over at death, we take with us the energy that makes up our true essence—the same way that we carried it with us in the physical. Dark energy caused by distressing issues that we experience here in the physical does not automatically disappear just because we have lost our physical body. We don't achieve automatic enlightenment just because we're dead.

* * * *

These issues are spiritual in nature, and we carry them with us when we transition into the spirit world.

Often, those issues do resolve themselves because the spirit world does offer help. My spirit guides have told me many times that some spirits take part in "therapy sessions" to help them overcome issues that are inhibiting them from progressing. "We are working with him," my guides will explain to me of such a soul.

Of course, these spirits have to be willing to work on their problems, just as they would here on Earth. For those spirits who do *not* want to accept help from others in the spirit world, these issues will remain and will distract their attention, causing the spirits to want to cling to the physical plane, where the issues first appeared and developed.

This contributes to the dark energy here on Earth. It makes no difference whether a person is physically present here on Earth or present on the Earth plane as a spirit—either way, the person's energy still contributes to the Earth plane's energy field and so affects the whole.

One of the reasons Lightworkers are incarnate on Earth is to help release such earthbound spirits, which, as we saw in Chapter 2, involves elevating the earthbound spirit's energy to accept more light and thus transforming the dark energy the spirit carries into light energy. The Earth plane is very heavy with these earthbound spirits right now, so there's a real need to release them and help them cross over into the light in order to help restore the Earth's energetic balance. This is why teachers on higher planes are activating so many Lightworkers in the form of "ghost hunters" and teams of "paranormal researchers" who help free the earthbound spirits.

## Addicted or Otherwise Maladapted Spirits

One of the most common types of spirits who hang around and become earthbound is spirits of people who were addicted to drugs or alcohol. Because humanity has become increasingly materialistic, we have many more spirits clinging to the physical in order to satisfy their leftover hunger for the material side of life. As previously explained, addictions, disorders, and even perverse behaviors are still present within the essence of a person's spirit, because these patterns are not only psychological and/or physical in nature, but they are also spiritual, as well.

These issues, coupled with a spirit's refusal to accept that he or she has died, will cause a spirit to try to satisfy these cravings here on Earth, because they can't be satisfied in the spirit realm. Even an addiction to cigarettes can cause spirits to remain behind and perhaps attach themselves to a smoker (who probably has no idea that it's happening) in an attempt to vicariously satisfy their addictive desires. But this strategy doesn't work because these spirits are no longer in physical bodies that react the same way to physical substances. The spirits remain frustrated and unhappy, and they find themselves stuck in a world where they no longer belong.

## Caretaker Spirits

Some spirits won't go until they can see their loved ones happy again. For example, my cousin cried night after night when her mother passed over. The two of them had been inseparable, and my cousin could not imagine how she would go on without her beloved mother. One night after crying herself to sleep, she dreamed of her mother. In the dream, her mother sat before her with a stern look, lifting her index finger and pointing it at my cousin. My cousin awoke and thought, "What have I done? My mother looks so angry with me!"

The next night, she again cried herself to sleep, and her mother appeared in her dreams once more with the same stern look. This time, when she awoke, my cousin understood the message. Her crying needed to stop. My aunt wanted her daughter to stop mourning so that everyone could heal and get on with their lives, including my deceased aunt.

This was a serious message not to linger in the grieving process. I suggested to my cousin that each night before she went to bed, she pray for both herself and her mother to be supported and guided through their respective processes. She found that doing this not only helped her through her grieving, but it also helped my aunt to be able to move on in the spirit realm. My cousin made a conscious effort to work through her grieving instead of staying stuck in it, and the visits eventually stopped. My aunt felt good about moving on and was no longer held back by her daughter's pain. She was always free to visit when she chose to, but was no longer held earthbound, trying to soothe her daughter's pain.

In my work as a medium, I've found that many spirits, just like my aunt, simply cannot move on until their loved ones have released them, and prayer can be a particularly effective way to help this process because it transforms dark energy into light and spiritually elevates all those involved in the process (both the person doing the praying and the person being prayed for).

Other spirits desperately want to connect with a relative to deliver an urgent message or to reveal unknown details about their deaths. Sometimes they become quite persistent, and often people who are not mediums will find themselves repeatedly dreaming of a loved one or experiencing strange occurrences (such as lights turning on by themselves or unexplained noises)—all attempts by the spirit to get attention so that the spirit can get his or her point across. If the loved one isn't able to decipher the message, he or she may have to visit a medium or other Lightworker for help communicating with the spirit so that the spirit can share his or her message and then be at peace.

## Permission-Seeking Spirits

I have also encountered many spirits who don't understand what has happened to them. When someone dies, the Light comes for him or her to help the spirit transition into the spirit realm. But if the spirit misses that opportunity the first time, the spirit can become lost and may need gentle guiding back to the Light.

### Saying Goodbye: Sophia's Story

One Saturday morning, I awoke to what sounded like the cry of a little girl calling, "Mommy!" Ever since my daughters were born, the slightest noise jolts me out of a sound sleep, and I've been known to hear even a cough through two closed bedroom doors. So when I heard the cry, I jumped up from my bed to check on Kara, who was six years old at the time. I found her sound asleep. Next, I checked on Rachel, who was sleeping comfortably in her crib. Perhaps I had been dreaming, I thought.

The very next morning, I dreamed that a little girl was standing beside my bed. When I awoke and opened my eyes, there she was—with her big blue eyes and long curly blonde hair—staring right into my face! "Help me find my mommy," she pleaded. I jumped up and squeezed my eyes shut, thinking I must still be dreaming. And when I opened them again, she was gone. Then I remembered what had happened the morning before, and I immediately knew that I had a lost little girl situation and that her spirit was trapped—confused and earthbound. I began to talk to her.

"Sweetheart," I said out loud, "I do not know your mommy or where she is, so please go find someone else to help you." Yet throughout the week, she continued to make appearances in my bedroom. I felt her presence all around me, and several times I heard her crying. As the days passed, I tried to enlist my guides to help her, but they told me she was resisting and wanted to stay with me. "But why?" I asked, confused. "I don't know her, and I don't know her mother. She can't stay here with me—she has to cross over." I wasn't getting any answers from my guides, and in the meantime, those big blue eyes were haunting me.

Then Wednesday rolled around. At that time, this was my day for doing readings at a local metaphysical shop. Usually, I took appointments, but I also took occasional walk-ins. On this Wednesday, I had two scheduled appointments and then stopped for a coffee break. The owner of the shop came to the back room where I was sitting and asked, "Got time for a walk-in?"

"Sure," I said. In came a blonde-haired woman clutching her purse and looking very nervous. It was obvious to me that she didn't normally visit psychic shops. As she sat down across the table from me, I was stunned at the first words that came out of her mouth. "Last year we lost our little girl," she said. "Can you contact her?" I nearly fell off my chair. As soon as the reading began, zoom! Into the room came this same little angel who had been trying to get me to help her all week long. I told the woman that her daughter knew she would come to see me and that the girl's spirit had been with me since Saturday. We dialogued for almost an hour. The little girl's name was Sophia, and she had been born with a genetic disease. The doctors did not expect her to live past the age of two, but somehow, she hung on until she turned eight. Mother and daughter had been very close until the girl's death a year ago, and ever since, the mother had suffered from such profound grief that she was basically unable to function. The reunion was incredibly emotional, and the mother wept as the presence of her daughter in the room became palpable. I cried, too, but I also laughed with both of them when they recounted how Sophia used to love to get into her mother's things and put on fashion shows in her room. "Your daughter is earthbound," I eventually explained to the mother. "It's time to release her."

"I couldn't let her go until I knew she was okay," the mother said through her tears. It was obvious to me that for her part, Sophia would not go without her mother's blessing either, and that she also needed reassurance that she would see her mother again.

We called in Sophia's paternal grandfather, who had crossed over years before and was nearby waiting to help, and we released Sophia to him. Her mother tearfully told Sophia that it was okay to go with her "Poppa," and that Mommy would be there soon. Thus assured, Sophia was finally ready. I became overwhelmed watching as grandfather and granddaughter held hands and then gracefully disappeared into a brilliant landscape of white light. When it was all over, Sophia's mother told me that it was the hardest thing she had ever done, but she knew she had to release her child.

* * * *

## Confused and Disoriented Spirits: Danny's Story

Another persistent type of spirit is the kind that crosses over traumatically after being ripped from the physical body without understanding what happened. (The scene in the book *The Lovely Bones,* as well as in the movie of the same name, where Susie's spirit runs away from her murderer, is a good illustration of this.) Just like little lost Sophia in the last example, these souls may be disoriented. It is like being suddenly transported to a foreign country where you don't speak the language and everyone ignores you; you have no idea what to do or where to go.

Sometimes these spirits see the deceased loved ones who come to help them, but the new spirits refuse to go with them because they don't understand that they have indeed died as well. Instead, they attach to the last person they saw in the physical—often the doctors, paramedics, firemen, police officers, or rescue workers who tried to save them. Although such emergency personnel rarely talk to anyone but trusted friends, family, and coworkers about this phenomenon, the truth is that many of them feel "haunted" in subtle and not-so-subtle ways by the victims they try to save. My husband Steve, now a detective with the New York City Police Department, had this happen to him many times when he was a patrol officer. He'd get up to 25 calls per shift, often rushing to a crime or accident scene where lives had been lost in the most violent and tragic ways. One particularly bad week stands out in my memory. Through scenes shown to me during mediation, as well as interviews my husband conducted, I learned Danny's story.

It started with a snowy January night when the roads were slick and many calls about accidents were coming in. As Steve was just starting his shift, a 17-year old boy named Danny who lived with his mother in one of the neighborhood walk-ups had been feeling antsy. He was tired of studying and didn't want to face the chore of filling out his college admission papers just yet. He called Mikey, who lived down the street and had been Danny's best friend since sixth grade. "Let's go for a ride," he pleaded to his friend. "Somewhere, anywhere, I just need to get out of here. I need a little change of scenery."

Agreeing to go, Mikey snuck out of his apartment the back way and hopped into his half-rusted green Honda. He pulled up in front of Danny's house a minute later. Danny flew down the snow-covered steps to meet him, ignoring his mother, who yelled behind him, "Where do you think you are going? The temperature is dropping and heavy snow is headed for us later tonight. A Nor'easter is coming in. You'll get in an accident if you go out!"

"She is always worried about something," Danny muttered, not bothering to zip his letterman jacket as he hopped in the car with Mikey, who had the heater already cranked to maximum and the music on loud. "Drive by Vanessa's house," Danny suggested, hoping to think of a reason to coax Vanessa out for a burger. He was working his way up to asking her to the prom in the spring.

Mikey laughed and floored it, screeching his tires as the car flew down the wet pavement. About 15 minutes later, he was reaching for a CD in the back of the car when an SUV pulled into his path. Mikey swerved on the now icy roads and managed to miss the SUV as Danny hung onto the dash. "That was close! Ya trying to kill me?" Danny joked, impressed with his friend's quick reaction. They headed towards Central Park West, with Mikey slowing down a bit,

* * * *

even though there was no traffic. On the car radio, the boys heard warnings about the impending storm.

"One hour with Vanessa and then we need to get back," Mikey said. He knew that he was probably going to get grounded for a week if his folks figured out that he snuck out again. He was imagining how he might try to sneak back in unnoticed when an oncoming vehicle's bright lights momentarily blinded him. Blinking hard, he did not see the BMW truck in his path.

"Holy..." he began to yell.

"*Mikey, look out!*" Danny screamed.

The sound of twisted metal and smashed glass filled the air. Mikey's car skidded and flipped over, smoke pouring out the back. "Dan...Danny!" Mikey yelled for what seemed like an eternity because the crushing metal sound never seemed to stop. Once the car came to a standstill, Mikey unclipped his seat belt and shimmied through his open window by sliding on his aching back. He heard no sound coming from Danny. His legs were shaking so badly that he had to crawl as he made his way to the other side of the car to look for his friend. What he found horrified him. Danny was convulsing, and his skin was as white as the snow that was now falling at a steady pace. "Get...get help," Danny whispered. "I can't feel....anything. Am I still alive?" Mikey reached in his pocket, praying that his cell phone was still there and hadn't been smashed. With shaking fingers, he punched in 911.

"I think my friend is dying! *He's dying!*" he yelled into the phone as tears ran down his cheeks. "You have to get here quick. You have to help him!" Steve and his partner were the first officers to arrive on the scene. "Is Danny okay?" Mikey cried as

Steve leaned down to check on the boy who was still inside the car, not moving. "Tell me Danny's going to be okay!" Crawling deeper into the car, Steve suddenly saw what a trained cop will usually recognize as a point of no return. Danny's neck was gushing blood, spraying with every beat of his heart, and there was a pool of blood underneath him. Danny had severed a major artery in his neck.

"Officer," Danny said in a shallow voice. "Help me...please. My ma is gonna be real worried."

"It's okay," Steve said, putting his arms around Danny's face and neck to warm him and attempt to stop the bleeding. Steve tried to keep the dying boy as calm as he could. "You're gonna be all right, buddy—just hang on."

"I gotta fill out my college entrance papers tonight or everyone is gonna be mad," Danny said.

"The ambulance is on its way," Steve said. "Just stay with me! Tell me about yourself. Do you play any sports?"

"Yeah, baseball. I think I might get a college scholarship,"

Danny said. "I think someday I'll...." As his voice trailed off, Danny died in Steve's arms.

## Here One Second, Gone the Next: Ben's Story

Two nights later, a call for help came in from a newlywed named Sally who lived on West End Avenue. Married for just six months, Sally and Benjamin had been getting ready to go out for dinner with Sally's parents. Ben had come home late, as usual, even though he'd promised Sally he'd get home early. Knowing Sally would be angry, Ben stopped on the street to buy her some $3 carnations—his way of saying he was sorry for never being on time.

"You better get in that shower!" Sally scolded when he walked in the door, hardly acknowledging the carnations.

"We've been late the last four times we've gone to dinner with Mom and Dad. You know how Dad is about eating late!"

Ben gave her a quick kiss and then jumped into their cramped little bathroom, which contained no more than a shower, a small sink, and a toilet—each within arm's reach of the other. Flipping on the hot water, Ben stripped, jumped in the shower, and soaped up his hair. He used that awful flowery shampoo that Sally kept on the ridge of the tub, and then he reached for his electric razor that was plugged in near the sink. When the soap from the shampoo fell into his eyes, Ben cursed and tried to rub it away. In the process, he dropped the shaver, and it fell into the water on the shower floor, instantly electrocuting him. A few minutes later, Sally forcefully opened the bathroom door to hurry her husband along. She found his body slumped on the shower floor, the water still running, and heard the loud buzzing of the hot, live razor. Hysterically sobbing, Sally called 911.

When Steve arrived, he could smell the still burning flesh from the hallway. He knew not to approach Ben's body because the water was still electrified. Realizing that that this young man had been alive one minute but instantly dead the next, Steve asked his partner to notify the superintendent to shut the power off.

"I am so sorry," Steve told Sally. "There was nothing any of us could have done."

## One More Fix: Nancy's Story

Four nights after Ben's death, Steve was on patrol when a call came in about trouble at an SRO (police lingo for a single-room occupancy hotel) in a lower income area of the city. Trouble at SROs was one of the worst possible types of calls because these places were often inhabited by drug addicts and other shady characters who lived in dilapidated rooms with virtually nothing to their names. On this night, a 40-year-old woman named Nancy—a former teacher turned drug addict—had taken a bad hit of heroin and called the front desk for help. Steve got there before the ambulance and knocked down her door. He found Nancy convulsing on the floor near her thin, dirty mattress. He could tell that she was not going to make it. Reaching out to him, Nancy whispered, "I made a mistake. I don't want to die." Steve held her hand and a minute later, she was gone.

## Helping the Helper

I try to make our home a sanctuary for my husband because he sees so much sadness on the job. Usually, he's able to shake off the events of the day. But after this particular string of tragedies, Steve began to have daily headaches and would wake up looking exhausted, even when he had had eight hours of sleep.

"Hun, are you coming down with something?" I asked him, but he shook his head."I don't think I'm getting sick," he told me, "but I've never felt so drained." Coming from a man who never complained about *anything*, this worried me.

* * * *

Weeks passed, and still the headaches wouldn't subside.

Steve began to look simply whipped. This athletic giant who could break through locked doors hardly had the energy to walk up our stairs to go to bed. One night, as I was turning off the light, he rolled over and confessed, "Sahvanna, I know something is wrong. On top of everything else that's going on with me, I keep having these strange dreams."

"What kind of dreams?" I asked.

"It's going to sound crazy," he said.

"Try me," I replied.

"Okay. I'm with all these people in a supermarket," he started. "Everyone is looking at me. They look familiar. I've seen them before, but I don't really remember who they are. One of them says to me, 'I don't know what to do.' The next one says, 'I don't know where to go.' Another one yells, 'You have to help me. I'm lost!'" Steve paused to take a deep breath. "Then I see the face of that boy," he continued, almost not wanting to say the next words. "You remember the one, right? He died in that car accident. He played baseball and wanted to go to college. His name was Danny."

I nodded, understanding. "And then do you see the face of the man in the shower?" I asked.

"Yes!" Steve said, a little amazed. "He's the one in the supermarket who talks about wanting to go back. He's saying something about meeting people for dinner. And then I see that...."

"Drug-addicted woman who took the bad heroin?" I said, finishing his sentence for him.

"Yeah! She's the one who tells me, 'I need a hit, where can I score?'" he said. "I keep telling all of them to go away and leave me alone. But they keep saying, 'We don't know what to do. Tell us what to do.' And the boy...well, he won't stop staring at me!" Then, in a voice that sounded completely wrung out, he said, "I'm so tired, Sahvanna." Although I was still concerned, I finally knew exactly what was happening to my husband, and I knew what I had to do to help him.

Steve had been the last one to connect with most of these poor souls before they faced sudden, violent, unexpected deaths. When they died, the one comfort that remained was the officer whose face was the last thing they saw, the man who had tried to help them and who seemed so strong and sure. (In Ben's case, even though he died instantly before Sally called 911, his confused spirit was still in the apartment when Steve arrived, trying to help.)

These spirits were earthbound, trapped because of the trauma of being abruptly ripped from their bodies. Instead of crossing over in a calm way and joining their friends and relatives who had already passed, they were confused about what had happened to their earthly life, wondering why no one seemed able to see them or hear them anymore. They didn't fully realize they were dead and so remained stuck between two realms, clinging to the person who came to help, hoping that he could somehow make things right again. They could not stop haunting his dreams, and their energetic demands were taking their toll on his physical body. "Steve, I think I can help you," I said, gently asking him to get out of bed and go with me into my office. Once there, I lit some candles, took his hand, and asked him to close his eyes as I continued to explain what was happening.

"The spirits of these people are attached to you because they want you to help them," I said. "That's why you're tired. They're taking your energy, draining you. They're chattering at you in your head and causing you to get those headaches. They don't allow you to get restful sleep at night. We need them to detach from you and cross over into the spirit world." I knew I had go into that zone where I could connect with them and try to help them. When I did, it didn't take long for me to sense how Danny felt trapped, how Ben was struggling with accepting the truth, and how Nancy was going through spiritual withdrawals from her addiction.

Calling in my own spirit guides, I asked them to find the earthbound spirits' loved ones to help them cross over. I figured that Danny, Ben, and Nancy were so traumatized that they'd never trust me enough to let me help them, but I was hoping I could get them to go with their loved ones and return with them to the light.

What followed was days of intense meditation and discussions with my guides, who were doing everything possible to right the situation. One found Danny's grandfather Louis in the afterlife and enlisted him to help find Danny and bring him gently to the other side. It didn't take long before another of my guides found Ben's friend Alex, who had died young of cancer and offered to take Ben by the hand and lead him on his new journey. The most poignant reunion occurred when

Nancy's mother came forward to embrace her daughter, helping her to see her true self as whole and addiction-free. All three of these earthbound spirits were finally ready to move on.

And as they did, Steve's headaches disappeared and he began to get his energy back. Soon, he was feeling like his old self again. The recurring dream about the supermarket went away and was replaced with Steve's usual dream of getting a call saying that the New York Giants needed him—and pronto.

## Sending Earthbound Spirits to the Light

As emergency workers do, Lightworkers often attract earthbound spirits, as well. Lightworkers do it inadvertently, drawing attention because of the extrasensory perceptions they possess. The earthbound spirits recognize that although everyone else seems to be ignoring them, the Lightworkers can often see and/or hear them. So they cling to the Lightworkers, hoping they can help them, just like the lost little girl kept coming back to me, asking me to find her mother. Fortunately, there's no need to be alarmed about such clinginess. As I said before, these spirits are not demons or negative entities, and although they can annoy you with headaches, fatigue, and bad dreams, they can't seriously hurt you.

If you find yourself or someone else feeling drained or unsettled because of a clinging spirit, shield yourself before you do anything else by envisioning a white light of protection surrounding you that is so strong that *nothing* can penetrate it. As you'll remember from the discussion of shielding in Chapter 5, this technique will keep you grounded and will prevent your energy field from absorbing negative energies. Do not forget this important step—in fact, it's vital that you as a Lightworker remember to shield yourself daily, just as you remember to buckle your seatbelt every time you get in the car. It's that important.

After you shield yourself, ask the spirit what the spirit's message is or what, if anything, the spirit may want to convey. Use the dialoguing method detailed in Chapter 15 to talk with the spirit and tell him or her that it is time to move on and that he or she does not belong in the physical world anymore. You may also want to enlist your own guides or deceased loved ones to meet with the earthbound spirit to explain what has happened and help guide the spirit back to the light so the spirit can cross over—the way my spirit guides found Danny's grandfather to help him go into the light.

At times, even when a Lightworker tries to help such spirits cross over, some refuse to leave; that's why shielding is so important. It will protect you as you continue trying to dialogue with the spirit (which might take several days or possibly even several weeks) until he or she eventually accepts what has happened and moves on.

## Assisting the Transition

If you are present when someone crosses over, explain to the person what is happening. Keep in mind that anyone who is near death is actually in a state of altered consciousness, including those who are delirious or comatose or those who are in advanced stages of dementia. Such people are usually more capable of interacting with both their outer and inner worlds than you might expect. As long as a physical body still has breath left in it, always assume that some level of consciousness is present and that the person can indeed hear and understand what you are saying on some level. That's why it's vital to talk to the person who is making his or her transition to prepare the person for the journey that is ahead. You might say that it's okay to go now and suggest that he or she look for the light and move toward it. Tell the person that his or her loved ones are there in the light, waiting with open arms.

If you know the names of the person's loved ones who are already in spirit, name them as you speak about them. If you sense that the dying person may be worried about those left behind, reassure the person that you will all be reunited in the spirit world one day and that everyone whom he or she leaves behind here on Earth will be okay. Tell the person that his or her family members are all willing to lovingly release the person into the white light. This is a very important step. My mother worked as a geriatric nurse for many years and has often seen deathbed patients clinging to life for days, just waiting for their grown children to arrive from other cities or states before they can pass in peace. Such patients needed to know that everyone was okay with their dying, and they needed a chance to say their goodbyes (even if they couldn't talk or weren't conscious).

Communicating with these people making their transitions can be done out loud or telepathically, which ever seems most appropriate or most comfortable for you. Because the physical body is fading, you will be communicating more on a spiritual level, so the need to say words out loud is not all that strong. If you are not present at the exact time of death or shortly before the death, you can still communicate with the person's spirit from wherever you may be at the time. The connection and bond of love and support that you share with the dying person will defy any geographical distance. After he or she has left the physical, continue to pray for your loved one and send positive light-inducing thoughts to help support him or her in the transition process.

You can use the same process for people you may not know personally, as well—such as after a natural disaster such as a hurricane or an earthquake that claimed many lives, or after a fatal tragedy like a school shooting or September 11th. Lightworkers often offer such assistance to the collective by sending prayers or light-inducing thoughts to all those affected. This works even when you don't have a personal connection with the people you are trying to help because as you read in the very first chapter of this book, we *all* share an energetic connection through Source.

After all, anytime Lightworkers take even the smallest action to spread love and hope on the planet, transmuting darkness into light, they are tapping into an energy that is far greater than most people could ever imagine. If you are part of this virtual Lightworker army that exists today, you are, though the grace of Source, serving as a channel for the Light—holding it, nurturing it, directing it, and using it for good in a world that is in desperate need of your service. Gently, but with enormous strength, this Lightworker army is using the many powerful tools and abilities outlined in this book to tip the scales and restore balance to a universe that is itself constantly evolving. The direction its evolution takes is entirely dependent on the amount and quality of light that we on Earth bring forward. As each Lightworker awakens to his or her path, that light expands exponentially— and nothing short of miracles occur.

# Epilogue

The messages in this book will ring true for so many; it is not easy being a Lightworker living here on the Earth at this time. The visions that I receive in meditation show that, at this time, the veil that separates the physical plane from the Astral plane is wearing very thin and is weighing heavily on our planet. This actually has so much to do with the energetic forces that we have created here on Earth. We are in the midst of a population explosion. At no time has the population of the Earth been so high.

As the Earth's population continues to increase, we seem to be going in the direction of more and more hatred, fear, and discontent, and many Earth inhabitants are harboring excess dark energy. When these dark spirits live out their lives on Earth and eventually transition, they do not simply disappear; their dark energy stays close to the Earth, and they inhabit the dark spaces of the Astral plane. Because these lower energies are materialistic in nature and lack spirituality, many will decide to reincarnate to enjoy more earthly pleasures, thus populating the Earth even more. As more and more of these dark energies are created and eventually transition, the weight upon the veil becomes heavy, and it wears thin as they wait to reincarnate. Perhaps one day some of these dark energies could actually break through, (as we discussed with vortexes).

As it bears down upon us, this dark energy lies heavily upon the Earth plane, like a trampoline holding too much weight. When that does happen, those on the Earth plane will not be introduced to heavenly angels or high-level beings, but many lower energy forms that cannot elevate their spirits past the first or second plane. It became necessary to allow many high-level beings to descend back to Earth. Making the ultimate sacrifice, these higher level teachers and light beings have agreed to come back to Earth to neutralize the darkness.

# Appendix

## Light-Inducting Affirmations

Recite a Lightworker affirmation each day to increase your light quotient. Any of these can be said at any given time or for any given circumstance.

1. I live each day to increase my light and that of the world.
2. All situations that occur are for the greater good of myself and all humanity.
3. Today, I am grateful for all that is good.
4. Being sick does not mean God/Source doesn't love me; recovery means I love myself.

5. My inner beauty is easy for everyone to see.
6. I am inspired to live my dreams and have faith that all is well.
7. I cannot fix everyone, but I can make a difference.
8. My Lightworker gifts are meant to heal, not hinder my own life.
9. I can only stay in the dark so long before I seek out the light.
10. I am a perfect petal on the flower that is humanity.
11. I do not worry because I know all is well with God/Source beside me.
12. It's perfectly okay to feel happy, safe, and secure.
13. All things in my life are in perfect balance and I live in harmony with all mankind.
14. I refuse to allow my light energy to be depleted by others.
15. I am here for a reason, and I will fully execute my purpose.
16. I accept myself and my own limitations.
17. I cannot heal others if they will not heal themselves.
18. It's okay to experience abundance in my life.
19. I accept myself for being imperfect.

20. I allow myself to fail and learn from the process of failure.

21. I am exactly where I am suppose to be at this time in my life.

22. God creates the map; I choose the roads I take.

23. I have free will to walk the path I choose.

24. My mind, body, and spirit are in perfect alignment.

25. I have complete faith in my inner knowing.

26. I will always find my way out of the darkness.

27. Retribution does not exist, only unconditional love does.

28. I will always have faith in the universe and its divine plan.

29. Fear creates dark energy; I refuse to live in the darkness.

30. I am free to pursue my divine mission.

31. Only I have the power to manifest the relationships I desire.

32. I accept my dark days, just as I do my light days.

33. My intuition is a gift from God/Source and I follow it without question.

34. It's okay to be praised.

35. I am a beacon of light for the world.

36. My hands are filled with healing energy, and I share it effortlessly with the world.
37. I am always safe in the light of God's/Source's love.
38. If I release my wishes to the universe, they will be returned to me in the proper form. The universe is always correct.
39. Today, I will make a conscious choice to not live in fear.
40. Today, I will consciously create more light energy in my life.
41. I place my ultimate fate in the hands of God/Source, and I know all is as it should be.
42. Today, I live in the light-inducing emotion of love.
43. I believe in the power of the collective and claim my part there.
44. Today, I will appreciate the skin I live in.
45. My physical body and spiritual self work harmoniously together to create the life I desire.
46. I affirm that we can achieve world peace.
47. All choices are my own to make. I reap what I sow.
48. I am always conscious of the divine guidance that is sent my way.
49. My body is the vessel of my soul, and I honor it.

50. I will be loved by those around me for who I am without conditions.

51. It's never too late to make things right.

52. Today, I will give my inner child a huge hug.

53. Today, I will make a conscious choice to appreciate and accept my flaws.

54. Today, I will stop and appreciate the beauty of the Earth and be thankful.

55. I will not take on the dark energies of those around me.

56. Today, I make a conscious choice to live in the light-inducing state of generosity.

57. I am always wrapped in a blanket of unconditional love by God/Source.

58. I release all that does not support my greatest good.

59. I cannot heal the world by myself, but I claim my part in the collective healing energy of the universe.

60. I can make a difference in my own life and the lives of others.

61. Today, I will make a conscious choice to forgive and not harbor ill will for anyone.

62. My greatest challenges have brought me only spiritual enlightenment.

63. I will love myself unconditionally and for all my shortcomings.

64. Today, I will send love and light to someone who hurt me.

65. When I overcome dark energy in my life, I transmute it for the entire planet as well.

66. Prayer is the highest form of self love.

67. If there were no dark night, we would never see the sunrise.

68. Today, I will make a conscious choice to forgive myself.

69. We are all neighbors in the community of mankind. Love thy neighbor.

70. Greed is just fear of lack in disguise. The universe is abundant and I will have all I ever need.

71. I remember that dark energy will only be transient in my life.

72. It is my choice to exit the dark; I stay as long as I choose.

73. Today, I will be a light in the darkness for myself and others.

74. Worry depletes my light energy; I will not give away my light to fear.

75. I am loved and supported in everything I do.

76. Not one good deed goes unnoticed by God/Source.

77. Let me be a guide; let my light guide those who are in darkness.
78. I love and cherish my inner child.
79. Hatred is just fear of loving yourself unconditionally.
80. Let me hold the torch for all humanity.
81. Love is all there is.
82. Energy never disappears, it transmutes. I can deflect dark energy easily.
83. I encompass all of God's/Source's healing gifts within myself.
84. My intuitive guidance is a gift from Source and I utilize it with gratitude.
85. It is perfectly okay for me to take care of me.
86. There is no such thing as failure, only a chance to begin again.
87. I always have free will to choose my own path.
88. Today, I will make a conscious choice to release any guilt I carry on my shoulders.
89. I have every right to happiness.
90. Let no person leave me without a good thought.
91. When I harm myself, I harm God/Source.
92. My light cannot be dimmed.
93. Today, I will talk to my inner child and tell him or her how wonderful he or she is.

94. Each day, I will pray for all humanity.

95. Source's light is my guide out of the dark night of the soul.

96. My body is perfect just the way it is.

97. Today, I will make a conscious choice to be there for someone who needs me.

98. Today, I will make a conscious choice of what type of energy I want to create my life with.

99. My loved ones in the spirit world are not far away. They love and support me always.

100. I offer myself the same compassion I would others.

101. I share my light with all those around me.

102. I allow myself to learn from my mistakes.

103. Today, I will make a conscious choice to make the world a better place.

104. I cannot judge others because I have not walked their path.

105. Source intelligence is always there for me to access.

106. I am never alone.

107. My creative abilities are heightened, and I will express them each day in some way, shape, or form.

108. Today, I will love and appreciate the magic of a child.

109. All events occur as a result of cause and effect, not divine retribution.

110. Today, I will make a conscious choice to release myself from any responsibility for any past abuse I have suffered.

111. Today, I will make a conscious choice to be tolerant of others' mistakes.

112. I can always recover what seems to be lost, because with God/Source nothing is ever really lost.

113. Today, I will not seek answers. I will seek the questions I need to ask.

114. No connection with another is ever in vain.

115. I cherish each experience in my soul's journey.

116. There is no good or bad within God's/Source's light, only love, and I live each day in that space.

117. Today, I will remember what it was like to be a child and appreciate life's small wonders.

118. Divine intervention is ongoing in my life at all times.

119. Today, I will make a conscious choice to keep all my relationships equitable and balanced.

120. Today, I will expand my light quotient by committing a simple good deed.

121. The bonds of love continue for all eternity and I am a part of this infinite blessing.

122. I am not afraid of intimacy and can share my emotions without fear of being rejected.

123. I will live each day with a deep sense of inner peace and love.

124. I can experience sadness as a healing experience.

125. Today, I will make a conscious choice to send love to someone from a distance.

126. I can make the difference just by being conscious of my thoughts.

127. I will always face what is true, even if it hurts me with the understanding it is for the greatest good of all.

128. My single prayer can heal the world; today I will pray for universal peace and love.

129. My spirit is a mirror image of God/Source; I will live each day in the light of that reflection.

130. Today, I will inspire others to not live in fear.

131. Today I will affirm that peace and harmony on Earth are possible.

132. Each time I send good wishes, I increase the light energy of the planet. Today I send good wishes to all mankind.

133. God/Source loves me unconditionally. I love myself without conditions.

134. I embrace my dark days and allow myself to feel each moment, healing and restoring myself with each moment.

135. I can see God's/Source's light in every child.

136. God/Source is the keeper of all my secrets; my pain is always exposed to God's/Source's healing light.

137. Today, I will make a conscious choice to practice self love and acceptance.

138. Moderation is the key to happiness. Each day, I will live in perfect balance with all the universe.

139. My addictions are symptoms of internal wounds that I can heal.

140. My internal dialogue speaks only of love and support for all I do.

141. God's/Source's healing power dwells within me; I heal my own life.

142. Today, I will make a conscious choice to open my heart to all possibilities.

143. Today I will make a conscious choice to face my challenges with courage.

144. Source intelligence is a part of me. I can access it whenever I choose.

145. I am all that ever was, is, and shall be. I am eternal.

146. I am shielded from all negativity.

147. There are no endings, just new beginnings.

148. With each stumbling block I overturn, I only grow stronger.

149. I have been here before, and I will return. I will plan accordingly.

150. I am the light in the darkness. There is no need to search.

151. I will meet my own needs first and then seek to help others. If I am wounded, I cannot help others.

152. Today I will make a conscious choice to keep my inner dialogue positive, loving, and supportive of all I do.

153. I am at peace with the universe and with myself.

154. I accept and trust the will of God/Source.

155. I have abundant energy and vitality for life.

156. Today, I will make a conscious choice to make someone smile.

157. It's okay to live each day feeling safe and secure.

158. My journey is eternal and I have a long way to go.

159. I allow myself to be imperfect.

160. Each good thought expands out into the universe for all eternity.

161. My uniqueness is what makes me special.

162. I can see the light side to life's mishaps.

163. Today I live in the light-inducing emotion of gratitude.

164. I am a part of the collective light energy of the universe.

165. I can be free to be myself where ever I go.

166. Unconditional love has no boundaries, so why should I?

167. Being over-sensitive is optimal to being void of emotion.

168. Today, I will make a conscious choice to not harbor the fears of all humanity.

169. Today, I will release any guilt I carry for any and all situations.

170. The wounds of my past are already healed.

171. Today, I live in the light-inducing emotion of forgiveness.

172. All my weaknesses are God's/Source's strengths, so I need not worry.

173. I am a perfect manifestation of God's/Source's love.

174. Today I will be a voice for someone who has none.

175. I will not support any fear-based media outlets.

176. Today I will encourage someone to follow his or her dreams.

177. I am complete and ready for my soulmate to come into my life.

178. I will not allow my empathy to bring unwarranted sadness into my life.

179. I can change my life.

180. Today I live in the light inducing emotion of generosity.

181. All the beauty of God/Source is stored within my soul.

182. Today I will make a conscious choice to release any outdated ideas or behaviors that do not support my greatest good.

183. I can enjoy my life without feeling guilty.

184. If one petal is damaged, the entire flower becomes flawed.

185. Acceptance is the key to contentment.

186. Today has all the power over tomorrow.

187. I will not attach myself to outcomes—only progress.

188. Today, I will make a conscious choice to follow my dreams.

189. I am a drop in the ocean, and I trust the tide.

190. I will not be afraid because the universe will provide all I need.

191. Divine guidance always surrounds me; I just need to recognize it.

192. My relationships enhance my life, not deplete my light.

193. Today, I will strengthen my faith system and trust that the universe is always supporting me.

194. I believe in the power of my light, and others will share my belief.

195. No matter where this journey takes me, I am grateful.

196. I nurture my dreams and give them all the nourishment they need to grow.

197. I am a healer, I will freely give my gifts.

198. Let me be the voice of hope and lend it to others who have none.

# Index

## A



## B



## C

# D



# E



# F



# G

## H



## I



## K



## L



## M

psychometry, 26, 82

# About the Author

Sahvanna Arienta is a practicing psychic medium and intuitive advisor with clientele from around the globe. A respected radio host and recipient of six International Paranormal Acknowledgment Awards, she has studied and explored the metaphysical and paranormal realms extensively for more than 20 years. She is also the creator of Soul's Journey Media, a New Thought company that brings messages of spiritual enlightenment to people all over the world.